Navigating Success Without Losing Each Other

A Self-Help Guide For Couples

Written By

Nfinda Teta Joao

Disclaimer

This book includes discussions on topics related to psychology, neuroscience, and mental health. While care has been taken to base this information on well-established research and sources, I am not a licensed psychologist, neuroscientist, or medical professional. The content is intended for general educational and informational purposes only and should not be taken as professional advice, diagnosis, or treatment.

Dedication

To all couples with high-achieving partners who face the challenges of busyness and miscommunication and find turbulence in the path of love and aspirations.

May you find comfort in knowing you are not alone.

This guide is for you to help illuminate the way and offer solutions for navigating success together without losing each other.

Your journey is important, and this book serves as a companion to strengthen your bond and guide you through your shared dreams.

Acknowledgment

I want to express my heartfelt gratitude to those who have supported me throughout this writing journey.

Firstly, I would like to thank God for His love and kindness and for guiding me throughout this entire process. I pray that this book reaches the hearts of those who need it most.

To my husband, who has been my rock. Your encouragement made this book possible. You have been there in my struggles and triumphs, and your belief in me has fueled my passion for this project.

To my daughter, thank you for your patience, love, and joy. Your warmth inspires me to be a better parent and partner every day.

To my family and friends, thank you for your love and support. Your encouragement has been a source of strength.

Lastly, I would like to thank the couples whose stories are in this book. Thank you for sharing your experiences. Your honesty and strength uplifted me, providing clarity on the challenges many face in balancing love and aspirations. I hope that each reader finds the inspiration to nurture their relationships and cultivate love as they pursue success.

About The Author

Nfinda Teta Joao is an author, marketer, pastor, songwriter, and entrepreneur from Luanda, Angola, now residing in the United States. She cherishes cooking for her family and spending quality time with them.

Her faith in God inspires most of her storytelling, with a focus on themes of hope and resilience. Nfinda holds a Bachelor of Arts in International Communication from Tshwane University of Technology, South Africa, and has contributed to two Portuguese anthologies: "A Escolhida," launched in Portugal in November 2024, and "Conexão Destino, a Protagonista," released in Brazil in April 2025.

In addition to her literary work, Nfinda released five hymns on platforms like Spotify and Apple Music. As an assistant pastor, she taught marriage preparation classes for five years.

Professionally, she spent nine years with the Public Finance Technology and Communication Service of Angola, where she managed communication and marketing and successfully rebranded the institute. Nfinda also holds a Digital Marketing Science Certificate from Texas Tech University, along with certifications in Google Ads and Google Analytics.

Connect with Nfinda: Instagram: @nfindajoao_official

Introduction

This book is inspired by my own experiences, which I want to share before we move forward.

I've been married for 15 years. I met my husband in Pretoria, South Africa, while we were both university students. He was pursuing a Bachelor of Science (BS) degree in Electrical Engineering, and I was finishing my Bachelor of Arts (BA) degree in International Communication. After my graduation, he decided to continue his studies and earned dual master's degrees, first in Telecommunications Technologies from Tshwane University of Technology and a second degree in Electronics and Telecommunications Engineering from ESIEE Paris. I remember he used to spend many nights studying at the university. One day, I jokingly asked him, "When we get married, will it always be like this?" He replied, "Of course not." Little did I know what was ahead!

When we got married, we started from scratch, but my husband was determined to work hard for our future. As the years went by, his work became more demanding. His main motivation was to create solutions that help improve people's lives. As a result of his hard work and determination, he became the first General Manager of the Angolan National Space Program Management Office, helping to design the beginning of the Angolan space program. This job required a lot of focus and often led to his absence due to frequent travel. At one point, he was away for almost a year, working on the launching of Angola's first satellite.

During this time, I had to take on extra responsibilities at home. I managed my career and our household while also taking on the dual roles of both mom and dad. I understood that his work was for our family's greater good.

Was it easy? No. There were many times I felt discouraged and misunderstood, and he also felt isolated and drained. Even though he was praised for his achievements, the challenges that came with success often made us feel disconnected—almost like strangers.

However, we strengthened our relationship by centering our marriage on faith and prioritizing communication, empathy, and mutual support. I realized that my first commitment was to God and that my role was to be a helper, not a hindrance. I began to recognize that my husband faced his own challenges, and I needed to provide emotional support to help him achieve his dreams. Today, he holds a Doctor of Engineering (D. Eng) degree in the Management of Complex and Large-Scale Projects from George Washington University, along with numerous other professional accomplishments, all for the glory of God.

This self-help book provides valuable tips for both partners on improving their relationship while addressing the unique challenges of demanding careers. It emphasizes the importance of couples understanding each other's pressures and offers guidance to couples on being supportive and empathetic. It aims to give practical strategies for navigating success together without losing each other.

I don't know what your situation is. You might be a senior pastor, CEO, scientist, or a leader's spouse. This book is for you. If you're a man or woman in a leadership position or a high achiever, this book is also for you. Overall, this book is for couples, regardless of your situation. Even if you're not facing the same challenges, this book can still serve as a guide for your future.

In the upcoming chapters, we will explore the cost of success, the importance of communication, the necessity of work-life balance, and the role of empathy in relationships. Together, we will learn how to align our personal goals with the shared aim of maintaining a loving and supportive partnership, making sure that neither love nor aspiration is compromised on our journey to success.

Table of Contents

Chapter 1: The Cost of Success 1

Chapter 2: Communication is Key... 15

Chapter 3: Establishing Work-Life Balance 35

Chapter 4: Building Empathy 44

Chapter 5: Supporting Each Other's Aspirations and Professional
Growth 56

Chapter 6: Surviving Work-Related Long-Distance Relationships
.... 69

Chapter 7: Parenting in the Pursuit of Success 79

Chapter 8: God as the Foundation of Your Relationship 90

Chapter 9: Practical Strategies for Reconnection 100

Chapter 10: Navigating Success as a Team 109

Conclusion 118

References/Sources 123

Chapter 1:
The Cost of Success

Success is most of the time seen as the ultimate goal in life. We are taught from a young age that we should dream big, work hard, and never give up, but we rarely stop to ask, "What does success really cost?" While ambition helps people grow and achieve great things, it also creates distance in relationships. Many hardworking individuals give everything to their careers while thinking that success will bring happiness, but during the process, they sometimes struggle in the one area they never expected, which is love.

For couples where one or both partners are deeply focused on their careers, work slowly weakens the connection that once felt effortless. Long hours at the office, late-night emails, and the constant pressure to succeed take away time that should be spent together. At first, ambition is inspiring. Therefore, watching a partner chase their dreams feels exciting and even reassuring, but over time, that same ambition turns into something else, something that makes the relationship feel neglected. Work always seems to come first, and love starts to take a backseat.

For example, Mark and Lisa were a couple who seemed to have everything. Mark was a senior executive at a growing tech company and he was known for his leadership and hard work. Lisa was a dedicated doctor who spent years building her medical career. They were both ambitious, admired each other's dedication, and felt proud of what they had accomplished, but as their careers progressed, their relationship began to suffer. Instead of date nights, they had work meetings. Their conversations became short and focused on responsibilities, such as bills, schedules, and daily tasks, instead of their dreams or feelings. Even when they were in the same room, they felt distant, as if their minds were always elsewhere. Neither of them planned for their relationship to suffer, but slowly, it did.

This happens a lot to people who are really focused on their careers. They want to be successful so much that they end up putting all their energy into work, leaving very little time for other things. Many people try to explain their long work hours by saying, "I'm doing this for us," or they believe that once they hit a certain goal, they'll have more time for their relationships. But the truth is, success is never a final stop. It just leads to new goals, more responsibilities, and even bigger expectations. Before they know it, couples start feeling like business partners instead of romantic partners. They might still love each other, live together, and have shared financial goals, but the deep emotional bond that once made them happy starts to fade. They go through life side by side but don't truly experience it together.

The loss of connection between two people doesn't happen all at once; it happens slowly over time. In the beginning, it might just be

2

missing a few dinners because of work. Then, vacations get postponed, date nights stop happening, and phone calls or emails start feeling more important than talking with your partner. As time passes, the emotional distance grows because one partner might start feeling lonely, even when the other is right there. Conversations that used to flow easily begin to feel like a burden, and the love and closeness that once made the relationship special start to fade little by little.

The real cost of success isn't measured in money or promotions; instead, it's measured in the moments that are lost. It's the birthdays that go uncelebrated, the quiet evenings that could have been spent together, and the deep emotional bond that weakens over time. No one sets out to let their career hurt their relationship, yet it happens to many well-meaning couples. Recognizing this issue is the first step to making a change. Success and love don't have to conflict with each other, but they both need careful balance. Achieving success in your career or personal life requires time, effort, and focus, but so does nurturing a loving, healthy relationship. When you dedicate too much energy to one, the other one suffers. To truly succeed and be happy, you need to balance both—your career goals and your relationships. It's important that your focus on success doesn't make you forget about the people you care about. You need to make time for both work and love so that neither one is left behind. By doing this, both grow and improve together. A fulfilling career is important, but so is maintaining a strong, loving connection with a partner. True success isn't just about professional achievements but it's also about having a relationship that stands the test of time.

Emotional disconnection happens when two people in a relationship stop feeling close to each other. It's not always about big fights or major problems, but sometimes, it's simply a slow fading of intimacy and warmth. A couple may still live together, share meals, and go through daily routines, but they no longer feel deeply connected. They may talk, but the conversations lack depth. They may be in the same room yet feel miles apart.

For many high-achieving individuals, emotional disconnection is not intentional. It often begins with long work hours, constant stress, and the pressure to succeed. Over time, the energy once dedicated to the relationship is drained by career demands. A partner who once greeted their loved one with excitement at the end of the day might now come home too tired to engage. The deep conversations between partners are replaced by work emails or phone calls, and being tired makes it easier to stay quiet; therefore, this gives another turn to the relationship. At first, it's just because of being busy, but over time, this becomes the usual way of interacting.

Imagine a couple who used to talk a lot about their day, but now they just send text messages. They may be too tired to talk after work, so they don't share their thoughts or feelings anymore. What began as a few busy days turned into a routine where they no longer communicate properly.

High levels of stress from work make communication difficult. A stressed mind is often overwhelmed, making it hard to listen, express emotions, or be present in the moment. One partner may feel too drained to talk about their day, while the other feels ignored. Over time, these small moments of missed connection build up. When couples stop sharing their thoughts, worries, and joys, they begin to feel like strangers rather than partners.

Emotional neglect is another major consequence of work-related stress. Neglect doesn't always mean a lack of love; it simply means that one or both partners are too preoccupied to show it. A spouse may no longer notice when their partner is feeling down, or they may forget to check in on how their day went. Simple gestures like holding hands, saying "I love you," or asking about each other's feelings become rare. This kind of neglect makes a person feel invisible in their own relationship.

When people start to emotionally drift apart, misunderstandings happen more often. Without good communication, even little problems grow into much bigger ones. It's easy for small things to be misinterpreted or ignored, and over time, these small issues cause more serious problems in the relationship. A partner working late might assume their spouse understands, while the other partner feels unimportant. A lack of emotional support leads to resentment, even if neither person intends to hurt the other. When couples no longer share their thoughts and feelings, they start making assumptions, often the wrong ones.

The psychological and emotional effects of disconnection are painful for both partners. One may feel lonely, even when their spouse is physically present. They might start questioning their importance in the relationship or wonder if their partner still cares. This loneliness leads to sadness, frustration, and even self-doubt. The other partner, often unaware of the depth of the issue, may feel frustrated by the growing distance but unsure of how to fix it.

Over time, emotional disconnection weakens the foundation of a relationship. Without attention and effort, the love that once felt effortless begins to fade. The good news is that emotional distance is not permanent; therefore, by recognizing the signs early and making conscious efforts to reconnect with your partner, couples may rebuild their bond. Moreover, understanding how stress, lack of communication, and emotional neglect contribute to disconnection is the first step toward healing and strengthening the relationship.

One of the most important steps in fixing emotional disconnection is recognizing when it's happening. Many people don't realize how much their work stress is affecting their relationships. They may think they are handling everything well, but their partner may feel ignored, lonely, or unimportant. Self-awareness means being honest with yourself about your feelings and actions. It is the key to understanding how work stress impacts your relationship. When a person is stressed, they may become short-tempered, distracted, or distant. They might stop noticing their partner's needs or emotions. Long hours at work leave little energy for deep conversations or quality time. Instead of feeling like a loving couple, partners start to feel like two people living separate lives under the same roof. The first step in fixing this problem is recognizing the signs.

Here are some questions to ask yourself to see if work stress is harming your relationship:

- Do I often come home too tired to have meaningful conversations with my partner?
- Am I easily irritated or impatient when my partner wants my attention?
- Do I spend more time thinking about work than about my relationship?
- Have I missed important moments (birthdays, anniversaries, or special events) because of work?
- Does my partner seem distant, frustrated, or less affectionate than before?

- Do we spend more time on our phones or laptops than talking to each other?

- Have our date nights or quality time become rare or nonexistent?

If you answered "yes" to many of these questions, then it is possible that work stress could be causing problems in your relationship. The good news is that realizing this is the first step to making things better. Once you understand what the issue is, you should start taking steps to fix it.

One of the best ways to reconnect is through open and honest communication. Many couples avoid talking about these issues because they don't want to argue or add more stress. However, avoiding the conversation only makes things worse. If one partner feels neglected or disconnected, they might start to withdraw emotionally, making the problem even bigger. Instead of letting that happen, couples should make time to talk about their feelings in a calm and supportive way.

When discussing these challenges, it's important to listen as much as you speak. Instead of blaming or accusing each other, you should try saying things like, "I've been feeling really stressed at work, and I realize it's affecting our time together. How do you feel about it?" Therefore, this opens the door for an honest discussion without making the other person defensive. Similarly, if your partner is the one who is struggling with stress, ask them how you can support them. Simple efforts, like checking in on each other's emotions or setting aside time to talk, make a big difference. Moreover, self-awareness and communication go hand in hand. The more aware you are of how work is affecting your relationship, the easier it is to make positive changes. Small steps like turning off work notifications during dinner, setting boundaries with work calls, or planning intentional quality time help couples reconnect. Recognizing the problem is only the beginning, while taking action to fix it is what truly strengthens a relationship.

Keeping a strong relationship while working a busy job is not always easy, but it can be done. Many couples struggle to find the right balance between work and love, often feeling like they have to pick one over the other. The truth is that success in both areas comes down to making good choices and setting priorities. Love doesn't grow on its own; it needs care and effort, just like a career does. Couples stay close while still working hard to reach their goals, and by practicing small but meaningful habits,

One of the best ways to balance work and love is by setting clear boundaries. Without boundaries, work takes over personal time, leaving little energy for a partner. Setting boundaries might mean stopping work emails after a certain time, avoiding work calls during dinner, or keeping weekends free for personal time. Talking about these boundaries with both a partner and coworkers helps to prevent work from interfering with the relationship.

Making time for each other is also important. Many people think love should be spontaneous, but when life gets busy, waiting for the right moment often means it never happens. Planning date nights, weekend trips, or even small daily activities like drinking coffee together helps couples stay connected. Quality time doesn't have to be expensive or fancy; it just needs to be intentional. Even spending 20 minutes each night talking without distractions makes a big difference. The key is to treat the relationship as a priority, just like an important meeting at work.

Good communication is another important part of balancing work and love. When people are stressed from work, they might not want to talk about their feelings, but keeping emotions inside creates distance. Checking in with each other daily is the best practice in this matter, and asking simple questions like, "How was your day?" or "Is something on your mind?" shows care and keeps the conversation going. It's also important to really listen, paying full attention instead of checking a phone or thinking about something else. When both partners feel heard and understood, they are less likely to feel ignored.

Small daily habits also help keep the relationship strong. Showing appreciation is one of the easiest but most powerful ways to make a partner feel loved. A simple "thank you" for making coffee, a compliment, or a kind text message means a lot. Another great habit is mindful conversation—looking into each other's eyes, holding hands, or giving a hug while talking. These small actions create warmth and closeness, even on stressful days.

For example, Maria and Luis used to take each other for granted because they were both focused on their careers. After realizing this, they started a habit of expressing gratitude every night. Before going to sleep, they each say one thing they appreciated about the other that day. It could be something big, like emotional support, or something small, like remembering to buy their favorite snack. This simple practice made them feel more valued and connected.

Balancing work and love is not about being perfect, but it's about being consistent. Some days, work will take up more time, but as long as both partners make an effort to reconnect, the relationship will stay strong. True success is not just about career achievements but also about building a life where love and ambition exist together. Many people believe that success and love cannot exist together, but this is not true. It is possible to have a great career and a strong relationship at the same time. The key is to work as a team, support each other's goals, and stay emotionally connected. Success does not have to come at the cost of love, and love does not have to stop someone from reaching their dreams. With the right mindset and effort, couples grow both professionally and personally without losing their bond.

One of the best ways to strengthen a relationship while pursuing success is by supporting each other's aspirations. Instead of seeing work as something that pulls them apart, couples choose to be each other's biggest cheerleaders. Encouraging words, celebrating achievements, and showing interest in each other's careers make a huge difference. Asking simple questions like, "How did your meeting go?" or "What are you excited about at work?" helps partners feel valued and understood.

Here are some key takeaways on how couples can stay connected and supportive despite their busy schedules:

- Take a moment to celebrate each other's wins, no matter how big or small. A simple text or a special dinner can make a huge difference in feeling supported and appreciated.
- Show your partner you value them by offering kind words of appreciation regularly. It doesn't take much, but it goes a long way in strengthening your bond.
- Even on the busiest days, send a quick message or make a call just to check in. It reminds them that you're thinking of them and that you care.
- Plan quality time together, even if it's just a small date night or a walk. It's important to reconnect and create those moments that are just yours.

- When you do have time to talk, make sure you're truly listening. Your undivided attention can mean more than you think in making your partner feel heard.

- Work on things together, whether it's a project or a future plan. Doing things as a team helps to keep that sense of togetherness alive.

- Be there when your partner is feeling stressed. Sometimes, just being a supportive listener or being a calm presence can make everything feel more manageable.

Moreover, couples should also be willing to adjust and grow together. Work demands will change, and life will bring new challenges, but the most successful relationships are those that adapt. Having regular conversations about needs, expectations, and future goals keeps both partners on the same page. Instead of waiting for problems to arise, couples who check in with each other often solve issues before they grow bigger.

Success and love are not opposites; they exist together with the right balance. No one has to choose between having a fulfilling career and a happy relationship. Therefore, by supporting each other, making time for emotional connection, and growing together, couples can build a life where both love and aspirations grow. The most rewarding success is not just measured in career achievements but in the strength of the relationships that make the journey worthwhile.

Chapter 2:
Communication is Key

Every close relationship starts with communication. It's how people show their love, work out their differences, and stay mentally close. Clear and honest communication makes both spouses feel appreciated and understood, but when it's lacking, even the closest ties start to seem far away. Communication is particularly difficult for busy people. Busy people have to follow deadlines, long hours, and tiredness, which usually leaves little time for in-depth discussions. These elements, over time, produce emotional detachment. Therefore, love does not vanish. Rather, couples lose their connection without regular and meaningful dialogues.

Good communication guarantees that both people feel understood and listened to, so it helps to create closer connections. It supports trust, helps to overcome problems, and maintains the relationship strong in the face of outside demands. Little misinterpretations become more serious without communication, which causes emotional distance, resentment, and dissatisfaction. A good relationship is about actually understanding one other, not only about spending time together. Open and honest communication leads one to that knowledge. Couples build strong emotional ties when they openly discuss their feelings, aspirations, and worries.

Still, communication goes beyond just chatting, and listening is also an important part of it. Many people believe they listen well when, in fact, they are just waiting for their moment to talk. Therefore, actively listening requires effort, which means being attentive, asking questions, and showing sympathy. Conversations take on an extra meaning when both spouses listen with understanding in mind.

Relationships suffer similarly under limited communication. One partner could believe the other feels the same way without sharing it. People may keep their small grudges to themselves until they become bigger. Discussions turn from meaningful to ordinary. This emotional distance over time causes the relationship to seem more like a convenience arrangement than a real connection. A person cannot experience emotional separation overnight. It develops slowly when communication breaks down. At first, it is minor, a spouse deciding not to discuss a difficult event from their day or an ignored simple misinterpretation, but these little events add up over time and widen the distance between spouses overnight.

A big problem with bad communication is that it leads to assumptions. People start filling in the blanks on their own when they stop having open conversations. If your partner isn't close to you after a long day at work, you might think they aren't interested.

Lack of compliments or words of affection could be taken as evidence that love is dying. Assumptions like these are often wrong, but they cause real problems when people don't talk to each other to clear things up. Still another problem is avoidance. Therefore, couples often avoid tough conversations because they don't want to fight. They keep issues under the carpet since they don't wish to fight. Avoidance, however, causes issues to grow rather than disappear. Avoiding tough talks over time results in bottled-up bitterness, which is far more harmful than a fight.

People with busy careers may feel like communication is another chore they need to do. Many people come home tired from a long day of meetings and work pressure, with little left for meaningful interactions. This tiredness causes emotional withdrawal. While one spouse may wish to discuss something significant, the other is too exhausted to participate. This starts a cycle whereby one person feels neglected, and the other feels under pressure to speak when they have nothing to offer.

Additionally, stress makes people angrier. A small problem that wouldn't usually lead to a fight turns into one because both people are emotionally drained. People who are stressed out and impatient tend to have tense conversations and miss the point more often. Another usual problem is being too busy with work. Someone could be thinking about their work even if they are sitting next to you. They might be checking their email, writing down things they need to do, or worrying about a project they need to finish soon. A true conversation becomes difficult when this occurs as one person isn't actually attentive. When a person isn't totally present at the moment, hence this lack of attention makes it challenging to connect or have a meaningful conversation.

Without any effort, work stress takes place over connecting with others. When this occurs, the relationship starts to seem more like an afterthought instead of a comfort and support system. People struggle with communication not because they lack interest but rather because their regular routines cause distance without their knowledge. The first step towards bettering communication is realizing these obstacles.

Finding time to talk is one of the hardest things for busy couples. When both couples have very hectic schedules, their talks usually last for a short time only. Most of the time, they discuss things like who will pick up the groceries or the next meeting's schedule. Even though these talks are important, they don't help you feel closer to each other. Couples start to feel less connected when they neglect to schedule time for more in-depth talks about their feelings or life events. Regularly failing to check in with one another could cause one to cease communicating their ideas and emotions. Therefore, it creates emotional distance.

People who are overwhelmed often withdraw rather than engage. People often just want to relax and be left alone at the end of a long, stressful day. Although this is reasonable, it makes a partner feel excluded or overlooked. Withdrawal slowly produces a pattern whereby deep conversations become rare. One partner quits sharing if they desire to spare the other from undue burden. The other might stop listening since they are too worn out to participate. Though they are still together, both eventually feel isolated in the marriage.

While social media and texting have made communication more easy, still both cannot replace in-person meetings. A quick question, "How was your day?" over text has less effect than a genuine chat. Messages, text, or email are difficult to grasp completely as they lack the tone of voice, facial expressions, or deeper emotions we typically acquire in face-to-face contact. Speaking with someone personally allows us to observe their expressions and hear their voice, therefore, it guides us to grasp their actual meaning. Without these, messages would seem flat or confusing, which would make the actual connection with the other person more difficult.

Misunderstanding is easy when people rely too much on digital communication like texting or emailing. Digital messages lack body language, facial emotions, or tone of voice, so the intended meaning may be misunderstood easily. Though that wasn't the goal, what might appear like a straightforward sentence in a book could come across as unpleasant or chilly. Without these nonverbal signals, one finds it more difficult to interpret the feelings underlying the words, which causes uncertainty or perhaps disagreement among people. This is particularly true in delicate or important talks when clarity and understanding are absolutely necessary.

Here are some non-verbal cues that help a partner understand when the other one is not feeling right:

- Lack of eye contact indicates discomfort or disengagement.
- Closed body language, such as crossing arms or legs, may convey defensiveness or emotional distance.
- A slumped posture might show sadness, fatigue, or lack of energy.
- Restlessness or fidgeting may show nervousness or uneasiness.
- Tight lips or a furrowed brow convey stress or irritation in facial expressions.
- Not wanting physical touch, like pulling away, could mean that you're feeling emotionally bad.
- A softer or more harsh voice tone could indicate disappointment or displeasure.
- Answers that are short or simple show that something is bothering them.
- Avoiding interaction or pulling away from the relationship could be a sign of emotional pain.

One common mistake in relationships is assuming that a partner automatically knows what the other person needs without talking about it.

For example, a person might expect their partner to know when they're sad, to help them when they need it, or to show appreciation in certain ways. However, if these needs aren't made clear, the partner may not understand, and those mental needs may not be met. Building a good relationship or meeting each other's expectations becomes challenging without open and honest dialogues.

Good communication means that both partners feel heard, appreciated, and connected, even though it doesn't mean always agreeing. Strong communication is thus what maintains partnerships healthy and strong. Without it, emotional distance, tension, and misunderstanding build gaps between spouses. Even with hectic schedules and professional obligations, the relationship gets stronger when both individuals try to be open, attentive, and explicit in expressing their needs.

Good communication is about really understanding each other rather than only exchanging words. Many couples battle this not because they lack love or effort but rather because they are not always conscious of the little adjustments that change their communication style. The way something is said, the tone behind it, and the ability to actually listen all help to determine how effectively couples relate.

Effective communication builds trust and emotional safety while also strengthening a connection. But when communication fails, misinterpretation rises, resentment deepens, and emotional distance grows.

I'm friends with a couple, Manish and Gildene, who have been married for seven years. I have had the pleasure of seeing their love develop despite the challenges that cultural and language differences present. Their love story is one of patience, understanding, and the joy of connecting outside of language.

Manish and Gildene are one of those couples you just know belong together. He's Indian, and she's Brazilian, but they both have living a lovely life. When they first met, it was almost like something out of a movie—Gildene didn't speak English, and Manish hardly knew Portuguese. You may expect it would have caused problems, yet it never prevented them from falling in love. They just somehow got one another. Their relationship strengthened with time, which shows that love only needs the correct hearts, not ideal words.

Of course, communication wasn't easy in the beginning for them. Manish often had to rely on translation apps to figure out what Gildene was saying. But even before he got better at Portuguese, she had already learned how to read him. She could tell how he was feeling just by looking at his face, the way he moved, the little habits he had. Moreover, by using gestures, facial expressions, and little acts that spoke louder than any words ever could, they created their own method of reaching one another.

Manish oversees a department at a travel agency and stays quite busy with his duties. Gildene, on the other hand, takes care of their home because of his job; stress follows him everywhere. She recalls him coming home after a long day, still on the phone, dealing with work even when he's supposed to be winding down.

That's where Gildene steps in with the sweetest little routine. She noticed early on that he often came home completely drained and starving, which only made his stress worse. So, for these particularly tough days, she came up with a simple but brilliant idea—she prepares a bowl of fresh fruit for him, hoping it provides a refreshing and comforting touch to help ease his stress.

The way she does it is so thoughtful. As soon as he steps inside, still deep in conversation with a co-worker, she quietly walks beside him, offering him pieces of fruit. She doesn't say much—just makes sure he eats. If he sits down, she sits with him, continuing to offer him small bites until he's done with his call. Though it takes little effort, it works as a miracle. He relaxes, his tension decreases, and for a while, the stress of the day disappears.

It's become something they do, a tradition that they don't say, but that means a lot. Gildene knows that love is about the small things, the subtle ways you express concern for someone, not only about big gestures. Her technique of saying, "I'm here, I see you, I love you," is how she peels an orange for him or offers him a piece of mango. Manish has grown to value these times as time has gone on.

Once he becomes comfortable, he starts to talk about his day, and I can tell how much he appreciates Gildene's company. She is always patient; she never hurries and listens him with patience. At times, all she does is hold his hand while he speaks, providing comfort without having to say anything. Overwhelming as his job may be, he knows that when he comes home, he has someone who understands him in a way no one else does.

Their love story is one that is truly inspiring. It's a reminder that genuine love is about being there for one another, day after day, in large and small ways, not only about passion and romance. Seven years later, they still take pleasure in these great times, hence deepening their relationship.

Active listening is a key part of talking to others, but it's more than just hearing what they say. Active listening involves truly attempting to grasp what your partner is saying instead of merely waiting for your chance to speak. People listen most of the time not because they want to understand but rather because they want to respond, which irritates one or both partners if they feel their voices are not being heard.

Active listening needs the whole focus. This involves maintaining eye contact, showing that you're listening by little verbal or physical signals like nodding or saying, "I understand," and shutting off distractions like phones or TV. A partner who feels really listened to is more inclined to express their ideas and emotions, therefore strengthening the emotional link between both of them.

Active listening calls for both reflection on and paraphrasing of emotions. This means repeating what the person said in your own words to show that you understand and reassure them that they've been heard. When one spouse says, "I had a really stressful day at work," the other might reply, "It sounds like today was overwhelming for you." This small act of reflection makes a great difference. It helps the speaker to avoid misunderstandings and gives them hope as their emotions are acknowledged. Likewise, clarifying inquiries helps one avoid presumptions. Asking, "What happened that made your day so stressful?" provides the speaker the time to more thoroughly describe their experience rather than reacting right away with advice or fixes. These little changes in communication style greatly increase the degree of connection between spouses.

Although listening is an important part of a relationship, so is clearly expressing demands in a way that allows understanding rather than conflict. Many relationship problems arise from not feeling heard or from expressing demands in a way that unintentionally sets off defensiveness. A common mistake is framing concerns as accusations. For example, telling someone, "You never help me with anything," is likely to make them defensive. On the other hand, telling them, "I'm feeling overwhelmed and would really appreciate your help," makes them more likely to work. Though little, the change is an important part. When emotions are framed in personal statements rather than blame, it prevents growth and keeps the conversation positive.

Vulnerability plays an important role in effective communication. It can be difficult to express personal needs, especially when past experiences have led to rejection or misunderstanding. However, sharing openly is essential for building emotional closeness. When one partner feels comfortable enough to say, "I feel lonely when we don't spend much time together," instead of simply acting distant or irritable, it opens up a meaningful conversation rather than creating conflict. Vulnerability creates connection, but it also calls for an environment of emotional safety where both parties feel confident sharing their ideas free from concern of rejection.

Beyond words, nonverbal communication is as effective in determining how partners see one another. Body language, such as facial expressions and tone of voice, all convey emotion, sometimes more strongly than the words being said. A person might say, "I'm fine," but if their arms are crossed, and their tone is cold, or else they are saying it with tiredness, then it's clear that something is wrong.

By noticing these body language signals, partners can better understand how the other person is feeling, even if words can't fully describe it.

Small actions that improve emotional connection are also forms of nonverbal communication. Simple touches on the arm, a friendly smile, or keeping eye contact during a conversation can convey unsaid signals of care and concern. On the other hand, the absence of these little gestures distances even if the words spoken are pleasant. This is why partners who are physically present but emotionally disconnected, such as checking their phones during conversations, often experience frustration. Giving full attention to even brief chats helps to build an emotional link.

Silence is another way people communicate without words, and it's easy to get the wrong idea from it. Silence sometimes indicates emotional hiding. But sometimes, it indicates someone is deeply in thought. If one partner stops talking all of a sudden after a conversation, the other person might think they are mad or not interested, which can cause extra stress. Rather than assuming anything, a straightforward inquiry like "Are you okay?" or "Is there something on your mind?" helps to avoid misunderstandings. Understanding the need for both verbal and nonverbal communication enables couples to engage in talks with more clarity and empathy.

For couples who prioritize their work, communication becomes difficult not because they don't want to connect but rather because time and resources are few. Conversations become transactional, narrowly focused on logistics like bills, schedules, or responsibilities, while emotional connection suffers as exhaustion sets in. It's therefore beneficial to check in often. Even short, intentional talks help to preserve emotional intimacy.

A daily check-in doesn't have to be long. It can be as straightforward as asking, "How was your day?" in a way that inspires a real response instead of a routine one. On the other hand, a weekly check-in goes deeper and lets both partners talk about any emotions or issues that might have been ignored during a hectic week. These times of connection help to prevent the growth of minor annoyances into more serious confrontations.

Little communication efforts help to maintain a strong relationship even during the busiest hours. A simple text message in the midst of the day, a voice note expressing gratitude, or a real "How are you feeling?" makes a big impact. It's about persistent, deliberate communication rather than about huge romantic gestures. When both spouses try to give communication top priority, misunderstandings go away, emotional connection improves, and the marriage stays strong despite the pressures of daily life.

Effective communication is about making a partner feel seen, heard, and valued. It's about creating an environment where both people feel safe expressing themselves without fear of being dismissed or judged. Relationships don't survive on love alone; communication is what keeps that love strong, even in the face of life's challenges.

There is another common issue that occurs with people who are very focused on their careers. High-stress professions need a lot of mental and emotional energy, which wears one out at the end of the day. Sadly, the tension from the job does not stay at work; it usually affects personal relationships. Usually, communication weakens when couples are exhausted, stressed, or preoccupied with their work. Rather than meaningful dialogues, they can distance themselves from one another, misinterpret what the other person says, or cut off all communication entirely. Even though they still love one another greatly, over time, this creates emotional distance between them. Maintaining a relationship strong and helpful depends on acknowledging how stress affects communication and working to solve it.

Stress has a direct impact on the brain and body, which also changes the way people interact with each other. When people face high-pressure situations, the brain's stress response is activated, releasing hormones like cortisol and adrenaline. These chemicals are useful for handling immediate challenges, but when stress becomes chronic, they interfere with emotional regulation and cognitive processing. This is why an overwhelmed person may become more irritable, less patient, or struggle to articulate their thoughts clearly. In relationships, this shows itself as short tempers, disengagement, or emotional shutdown. A spouse who seems far-off or apathetic could not be losing interest in the relationship; rather, they could be trying to control their emotions under pressure. Therefore, understanding this difference helps to avoid pointless misinterpretation.

Effective management of stress helps to prevent disruptions in communication. Some people avoid challenging talks because they believe they would simply worsen their stress. Others might become reactive, showing annoyance in ways that might seem to be defensiveness or criticism. None of these strategies encourages good communication. Stress should so be identified and controlled actively instead. Before having important conversations, couples should make sure they are checking in with themselves. Taking a few minutes to decompress—deep breathing, a quick stroll, or a quiet moment of introspection, helps to avoid emotions from getting out of control if stress is severe.

In addition to managing stress, setting boundaries is important for protecting relationship time. A lot of workers have trouble separating their work and personal lives, especially if they have jobs that require them to be available all the time. Work affects personal time without defined boundaries, thereby leaving little opportunity for real connection. Creating work-free zones, like keeping laptops and phones away from the dinner table or designating specific hours as tech-free helps couples concentrate just on each other. These little adjustments help to point out the value of their time together and the need not to let outside distractions break it.

Another important boundary involves how work-related stress is communicated. Although it's normal to want to let a spouse know about problems, continuous venting without a solution creates negativity. Couples establish rules for talking about work in a way that is useful rather than draining instead of letting job stress rule interactions. You should set out a certain period, let's say ten minutes to discuss frustrations connected to your job and make sure the evening is not overshadowed by the chat. After this set period, turning the emphasis to something constructive. Such as common hobbies or accessible activities, helps to prevent work-related stress from controlling the relationship.

Any relationship will have conflict, but how those conflicts are resolved makes all the difference. Stress sometimes increases problems, which allows the escalation of little conflicts into more serious conflicts. Pausing before responding helps to avoid needless anxiety when emotions are running strong. Stepping aside for a while helps both partners to gather their ideas and approach the discussion with a better perspective if a conflict gets more intense.

Healthy resolution of problems depends on compromise and mutual understanding. In high-pressure careers, it's common for schedules to clash, leading to frustrations overtime management and priorities. Changing the focus from who is right or wrong to solving problems would help both spouses support cooperation. This can include changing plans, assigning tasks, or merely appreciating one another's work. A partnership is about finding balance and helping each other through difficult situations; it is not about winning arguments.

After an argument, taking steps to repair the emotional disconnect is important. Apologies should be real and concentrate not only on the words but also on the behavior that follows. Sometimes, trust can be rebuilt only by a basic recognition of the emotions of the other person. Phrases like, "I understand why you felt that way" or "I didn't mean to make you feel unimportant" go a long way in reaffirming emotional security. Instead of allowing unresolved tension to remain, careful and sympathetic resolution of problems helps avoid resentment developing over time.

Developing a regular communication schedule helps one to remain connected even with hectic schedules. Emotional connection is strengthened by little and deliberate behaviors, including sending a nice note during the day, sharing one positive thing about each other before bed, or spending a few minutes each night checking in with one another. Though it takes little time, these routines establish a pattern of connection that keeps the relationship strong.

Every couple's communication style is different, and strategies should be adapted to fit their special needs. While evenings may be more successful for some, morning talks over coffee could be the ideal setting for others to bond. The secret is to be intentional about keeping in touch even in hectic lives.

In communication, growth is continuous. There will always be times of miscommunication or irritation since no couple runs flawlessly all the time. What counts is the will to keep becoming better and grow from every event.

A good and happy relationship depends on daily improvement of communication with your partner.

These six straightforward ideas will help you improve your everyday talks:

- Be present and avoid clear of distractions, like TV or phones, during discussions. This makes you connect better and shows respect.
- Avoid phrases to put the blame on your partner. Speak from your emotions and wants using "I" words. Say, for instance, "I feel upset because of something you did," instead of "You always make me feel like this..." This promotes understanding and helps prevent guilt.

- Give your whole attention, exhibit empathy, and reassure them you have understood to develop active listening.

- Decide when to schedule important meetings. To make sure the discussion is more successful, both of you should be composed and free from outside distractions.

- Schedule time often to follow up with one another regarding your emotions, worries, and valued items. This helps stop increasing issues.

- Show daily gratitude for the positive traits or daily efforts of your spouse. Your relationship will benefit much from small acts of thanks.

Couples who actively improve their communication abilities may build a relationship that is not only strong under pressure but also very satisfying. Additionally, couples can keep a supportive relationship going no matter what their working obligations are by dealing with stress, setting limits, resolving disagreements in a healthy way, and developing regular communication habits. When communication takes the front stage, love stays a source of strength instead of a victim of stress.

Chapter 3:
Establishing Work-Life Balance

Balancing work and personal life is not easy, especially for people who are very focused on their careers. When you work long hours and have a lot of responsibilities, it's hard to find time for your family, partner, and other people around you.

When you don't have clear boundaries, then work takes over your life. You might find yourself always thinking about work, even when you are at home or with your loved ones. This causes stress and makes it harder to connect with the people you care about. It's important to set limits that help you separate work from personal time. When you have boundaries in place, you relax and enjoy time away from work, which helps reduce stress.

One of the simplest ways to create boundaries is by unplugging from work after your workday is done. This means turning off your work phone or email and not checking work messages when you're at home. It might feel hard at first, but it's really important to give yourself time to relax and enjoy life outside of work. If you don't do this, stress from work starts to affect your relationships, and it can be hard to focus on anything other than work.

If you work remotely, then it isn't easy to separate your work and personal life. There's a good way to do it, and that's by creating a special space just for work. When you're in that space, you'll know it's time to focus on work, and when you leave that space, you focus on relaxing and spending time with others. This helps you mentally switch from work mode to home mode.

Another way to set boundaries is by setting time limits for how long you will work each day. For example, when you decide that after certain hours, you won't be able to work anymore and you need a break. This will give you time to relax, have dinner, and spend time with your loved ones. Setting limits for your workday helps you make sure you have enough time to take care of yourself and the people who are important to you.

Moreover, it is also helpful to plan time for yourself and your personal life. Just like you schedule meetings and work tasks, you should schedule time to rest or do things you enjoy. When you plan this personal time, it helps make sure that work won't take over your life. Having time for yourself will also help prevent burnout, so you can be more productive at work when you do focus on it.

Setting boundaries is another effective way to maintain a work-life balance. When you create limits, you'll feel like you have more control over your time. You'll know when it's time to work and when it's time to relax. This makes you feel less stressed and allows you to focus better when you're at work. You'll also have more energy to spend with your loved ones, which will improve your relationships.

Sometimes, work still feels overwhelming, and you might feel like you need to answer emails or take calls even after hours. In these moments, it's important to talk to your boss or coworkers and let them know when you're available and when you need personal time. Communicating your boundaries helps others respect your time, and they may even understand that you need time away from work to recharge.

Some people might feel guilty for taking time away from work, especially if they feel like they are letting others down. However, it's important to remember that taking care of yourself and spending time with loved ones is just as important as your job. When you take care of yourself, you'll be able to do a better job at work. In the long run, setting boundaries will help you succeed in both your career and your personal life.

Managing stress is very important to keep your work and personal life different, especially when you have a demanding job. High-pressure jobs make you feel very stressed, and if this stress isn't managed, it leads to burnout. Burnout is when you feel completely exhausted and can't keep going. When this happens, it hurts your emotional connection with your partner. If work stress is not dealt with, it causes problems in your relationship.

Stress builds up quickly when you have a lot to do at work. Long hours and tight deadlines make you feel overwhelmed. This affects how you feel and how you act. When you're stressed, it's hard to focus on your partner or to enjoy your time together. If you keep working without taking a break, you may start to feel emotionally drained, which leads to exhaustion.

The first step in managing stress is to notice when it is starting to affect you. When you feel anxious, tired, or unable to focus, it might be a sign that you are stressed. It's important to recognize these feelings early before they get worse. If you ignore stress, it will keep building up, making it harder to connect with your partner and causing more problems. Therefore, paying attention to your stress and dealing with it prevents burnout and keeps your emotional bond strong.

Once you know that you are stressed, it's time to do something about it. However, there are many ways to reduce stress, but here are some helpful ideas:

- Many people find that physical activity helps them relax. Exercise releases endorphins, which are chemicals that make you feel happier and less stressed. It also helps clear your mind so you focus better. Whether it's going for a walk, running, swimming, or doing another type of exercise, moving your body improves your mood and makes it easier to handle work pressure.

- Taking deep, slow breaths helps reduce stress right away. It helps slow down your heart rate and calms your mind. Try taking a few minutes each day to practice deep breathing. Inhale deeply for four seconds, hold your breath for four seconds, and then exhale slowly for four seconds. This simple technique will help you feel more relaxed and focused.

- Getting a good night's sleep is one of the best ways to reset your mind and body. When you're well-rested, you're better able to handle stress, think clearly, and stay emotionally balanced. Try to stick to a regular sleep schedule and create a relaxing bedtime routine to help reduce stress.

- Playing with kids makes you laugh, or just watching children play lifts your mood instantly. Laughter triggers the release of feel-good chemicals in the brain and helps you feel more connected and relaxed. Taking a break for fun with children is an instant healing.

- It's important to take breaks throughout the day. Whether you're working at your desk or at home, stepping away from your work for a short time helps clear your mind and reduce stress. Take a short walk, have a cup of tea, or just step outside for fresh air.

These small breaks help you recharge and feel less overwhelmed.

- Writing down your thoughts helps you manage stress. Sometimes, putting your worries on paper makes them feel less overwhelming. You can write about what's causing stress, how you're feeling, or what you're grateful for. This practice helps you process your emotions and clear your mind.

Taking a few minutes each day to relax and focus on yourself helps you feel more calm and balanced. These activities help you manage stress and be more focused at work, which also makes it easier to be present with your partner.

It's also important to talk openly with your partner about stress. If work is getting overwhelming, it helps to share your feelings. Talking about your stress makes it easier for your partner to understand what you are going through and offer support. This communication will help both of you feel more connected and give you a chance to find solutions together. For example, if you are too busy at work, you and your partner can discuss ways to adjust your schedule or take more time to relax. When you talk about stress, your partner might help you find ways to manage it while making it easier to stay close.

Keeping intimacy in your relationship is also important for managing stress. Intimacy is not just about physical closeness but also about emotional connection. When stress takes over, it's easy to let intimacy slide. However, making time for intimacy is important. Small actions like holding hands, talking about your day, or spending time together help you feel closer to your partner. These little moments reduce stress and strengthen your bond.

Finding a balance between work and personal life is not something that happens quickly. It takes time, effort, and communication. You may need to try different ways to manage your time and stress. But it's important to remember that you don't have to choose between being successful at work and having a happy relationship. You will have both if you set clear boundaries, manage stress, and make your relationship a priority.

Even if your job is demanding, making time for your partner is still possible. For example, scheduling regular date nights or setting aside time for meaningful conversations helps keep the relationship strong. When you make time for each other, you stay connected and support each other, even when life gets busy.

Managing stress and balancing both work and personal life requires making intentional choices. One important skill in achieving this balance is learning to say no. It's not always easy, especially for people who feel the need to please others or fear missing out on opportunities. However, saying no is essential for protecting your time, energy, and relationships. In this section, we'll explore the importance of saying no, how it helps reduce stress, and practical ways to start saying no without feeling guilty or overwhelmed. By learning this skill, you create space for what matters most and avoid burnout while ensuring both your career and personal life thrive.

Saying "no" is an important part of managing your time and reducing stress. It helps you avoid overcommitting and makes sure you don't do more than your capacity. Here are some ways that help you to practice and say "no" to a few situations or things:

- You should understand when you're reaching your limits, whether it's with work, social obligations, or other commitments. Saying "no" allows you to protect your time and energy, giving you space for your relationship and self-care.

- When you need to say "no," be honest but kind. You don't need to give a long explanation—you may simply say, "I'm unable to take this on right now," that is enough. Being clear and direct helps set boundaries without guilt.

- Learn that it's okay to put yourself and your loved ones first. Saying no to extra work or events when you need rest or time with your partner helps maintain balance and reduces burnout.

- If you struggle with saying no, practice it in small situations. The more you practice, the easier it becomes to protect your time without feeling guilty.

- Remember that just because someone asks you to do something doesn't mean you have to say yes. It's okay to say no without feeling like you're letting anyone down. For example, if you're asked to stay late or take on more tasks than you handle, politely decline if it will interfere with your time. Setting clear work boundaries helps you avoid burnout and keep a healthy balance.

Learning to say no is important for managing your time effectively and protecting your relationship. It allows you to create space for what matters most and maintain a healthier, more balanced life. By saying no when necessary, you ensure that both your career and your relationship get the attention they deserve.

At the end of the day, it is all about finding a balance that works for you. These things will always be part of life, but learning how to handle them will make a big difference in your well-being and your relationship.

Chapter 4:
Building Empathy

Empathy is the deep emotional connection that helps two people feel seen, heard, and understood. In any relationship, especially romantic ones, it is a powerful thing that brings people closer. When partners show empathy, they are not just listening with their ears, but they are also listening with their hearts. They try to feel what the other person is feeling, even if they don't fully understand the situation. This kind of understanding builds trust, closeness, and emotional safety.

In a strong relationship, each person wants to feel like their emotions matter. They want to know that when they are sad, angry, stressed, or happy, their partner is with them, not to fix things, but simply to care. Empathy makes that possible. It creates a space where both people express themselves without fear of being judged or ignored. Even small moments of empathy bring healing. A kind word, a gentle tone, or just listening patiently makes a big difference in how connected two people feel.

Often, people think empathy means agreeing with someone, but that's not true. Empathy is about understanding where someone is coming from, even if you don't share their opinion. It's about saying,

"I see why you feel that way," not necessarily, "I feel the same way." This difference matters, especially during tough conversations. If one person feels hurt and the other quickly defends themselves, then the hurt deepens. But if the other person responds with calm and tries to understand the emotion behind the words, healing begins. The act of being understood is powerful. It softens anger, eases stress, and rebuilds connection.

Sometimes, people confuse empathy with sympathy. Sympathy is feeling sorry for someone, often from a distance. Empathy is standing beside them emotionally and saying, "I'm with you in this." For example, if someone comes home and says, "I had a terrible day at work," sympathy might sound like, "That sucks." But empathy would sound like, "That must have been really hard. Do you want to talk about it?" The second response invites closeness. It opens the door to connection.

Still, empathy isn't always easy. Many things get in the way, and one major block is a distraction. Mostly, people are busy, tired, or looking at their phones. When one partner tries to talk, the other might not be fully present. Without attention, there will be no empathy. Another block is defensiveness. When someone feels blamed or criticized, they often shut down or argue instead of trying to understand. Past emotional wounds also make it hard to be empathetic. If a person has been hurt before, they might protect themselves by avoiding deep emotions, even in a current relationship.

But the good news is that empathy can be learned. It doesn't come only from natural talent; it comes from practice. The first step is to become a better listener. This means putting away distractions, making eye contact, and really focusing on what the other person is saying. It also means not interrupting or jumping in with advice too soon. Instead, the listener should try to hear the feelings behind the words. Asking thoughtful questions also deepens empathy. Instead of giving advice, a partner might ask, "How did that make you feel?" or "Do you want me to do anything for you?" These kinds of questions show care and interest. They also make it easier for the other person to open up.

Validating emotions is another important part of empathy. Validation means saying, "I get it," even if you would have reacted differently. It's saying, "That makes sense," or "I understand why you'd feel that way." These small phrases might calm tension and help the other person feel safe. When people feel safe, they share more. And when they share more, the connection grows.

Empathy is also about small actions. A gentle touch, a thoughtful message, or simply sitting together in silence. Sometimes, empathy means holding back your own feelings for a moment so you focus on your partner's. This doesn't mean ignoring your own needs; it just means choosing the right time to share them. If both people had a rough day, it might help if one listens first and then takes a turn to share. Taking turns builds mutual care.

Moreover, couples also need to understand their own emotions to give empathy to their other half. This is called self-empathy. If someone is burned out or stressed, they might snap or withdraw instead of listening with care. But when they pause and ask themselves, "What am I feeling?" or "What do I need right now?" they calm themselves and come back to the conversation with more understanding. Self-awareness makes empathy easier.

Even in conflict, empathy helps. Instead of focusing on who's right or wrong, partners should ask each other, "What are you feeling?" or "What do you need from me at this moment?" These questions turn arguments into conversations. They shift the goal from winning to connecting, and when people feel heard, they're more willing to listen in return.

Over time, empathy becomes part of the relationship's foundation. It makes both people feel valued and respected. It helps them face life's ups and downs as a team. Even when things are hard, like job loss, illness, or stress—empathy makes it easier to stay connected. It reminds each person that they are not alone.

In every relationship, there are moments when life feels heavy, when work becomes overwhelming, when family pressures rise, or when personal challenges appear without warning. During these times, the emotional strength of a couple is truly tested. One of the most meaningful ways partners support each other is by offering emotional care. This care isn't about solving problems but about standing beside each other with patience and understanding.

When one partner is going through something difficult, their emotions may show up in different ways. They may become quiet, short-tempered, tearful, or seem distant. It's important for the other partner to notice these signs early. Recognizing emotional shifts takes attention. It means paying close enough attention to see when something feels off, even before words are spoken. A simple observation like, "You don't seem like yourself today," opens the door to an important conversation.

Responding to emotions with care takes practice. The most helpful thing a partner should do in these moments is to stay calm and kind. Instead of asking, "What's wrong with you?" you should ask, "Do you want to talk about what's going on?" This small shift in tone shows concern instead of pressure. People open up more when they feel safe, not judged or rushed. Gentle questions and quiet patience often bring more comfort than loud advice or quick opinions.

Sometimes, the person struggling may not want to talk right away and that's okay. Emotional support doesn't always mean having deep conversations. It also means sitting together in silence, offering a warm hug, or giving space when needed. What matters is being emotionally available and letting the other person know they are not alone and that they matter. This kind of presence builds deep emotional security over time.

Here are some additional pointers that align with and enhance this context:

- Maintain gentle eye contact. A soft gaze conveys attentiveness and empathy without the need for words. Eye contact is the main nonverbal way of indicating engagement, interest, attention, and involvement.

- You may offer a comforting touch. A simple gesture, like holding hands or a reassuring pat on the back, provides significant emotional support. Touch is a form of nonverbal communication that promotes physical and psychological well-being.

- Be physically present. Sometimes, just being there, sitting nearby, or sharing the same space offers immense comfort. This presence communicates support and understanding without the necessity of conversation.

- You should respect their need for silence. Allowing your partner the space to process their emotions without pressure to speak can be a profound form of support. It shows patience and respect for their emotional state.

- Use facial expressions to convey empathy. A compassionate smile or a concerned look expresses understanding and solidarity. Facial expressions are a key component of nonverbal communication, conveying emotions effectively.

These nonverbal cues are powerful tools in providing emotional support, reinforcing the bond between partners, and nurturing a sense of security and understanding.

One powerful way to show support is to match the level of emotion being shared. If a partner is upset, brushing it off or staying too quiet, feel dismissive. On the other hand, reacting with too much intensity makes things worse. The goal is to meet each other in the middle— matching tone, pace, and energy so that the emotional space feels balanced and safe.

It's also helpful to listen without jumping to solutions. Many people want to fix things right away when their loved one is in pain. But sometimes the most comforting response is, "I'm here for you," or "That sounds really hard." These simple words show emotional presence. They help the person feel seen, which is often more healing than advice.

Emotional support also means being consistent. Showing care during one tough moment is good, but showing up again and again builds lasting trust. Even just checking in later with, "How are you doing today?" shows that the person's feelings didn't go unnoticed.

It proves that their emotions matter long after the moment has passed.

Partners should also learn each other's emotional styles. Everyone expresses stress and sadness differently. One person may want to talk through every detail, while the other may need time to think before sharing. Understanding how each person handles hard emotions helps avoid misunderstandings. It's important to remember that giving emotional support doesn't mean taking on the other person's pain completely. It means walking beside them, not carrying their burden alone. A healthy partner knows how to care deeply without losing themselves in the process. They stay kind and supportive while also looking after their own emotional health.

Boundaries play a role in emotional support, too. If a partner is feeling drained or overwhelmed, it's okay to say, "I want to be here for you, but I also need a little time to recharge." Honest communication like this keeps both people emotionally safe. It allows support to flow both ways, instead of one person always giving and the other always receiving.

The goal is to create a partnership where both people feel emotionally connected. When stress hits one, the other becomes the anchor. And when the roles reverse, that same care is returned. This emotional teamwork makes relationships stronger and more able to face life's challenges.

At the same time, emotional support means celebrating joyful emotions, too. When one partner is excited, proud, or hopeful, the other should be there to cheer them on. Sharing in happiness is just as important as sharing in pain. Both types of emotional connection build a rich and supportive bond.

Moreover, when you look at things through the eyes of your partner, you understand how they feel without making the situation about you. If your partner tells you they feel lonely even though you're home every night, you might want to make a list of all the ways you've been there for them. When you show empathy, you look for the kind of connection they long for. Therefore, it becomes easier for people to understand how their partner might be feeling when they try to picture it in terms of their personality, background, or emotional needs. This brings people closer.

Seeing things from their point of view also helps when you disagree with them. The question "What matters most to them right now?" takes priority over "Who is right or wrong?" Better, more loving talks start with that small change. It proves that love always wins, even when things are tense. Repeating phrases to show that you have heard them, like "So, you're saying you felt overwhelmed at work?" Therefore, doing so makes your partner feel deeply heard.

There are a lot of shared chores, emotional duties, and life duties that come with being in a relationship. Depending on health, work, family needs, or other changes, these jobs often change over time. If one or both partners feel like their efforts are not being seen or are not being matched, problems get worse. That's why it's important to know not only what each person does but also how that job makes them feel.

There are times when one person does most of the housework, and the other makes most of the money. Both jobs are important, but it gets annoying when one person feels like they aren't being helped. Being honest about jobs helps build trust and understanding. It also helps people switch places in their minds for a moment. Questions like "What's your day like most of the time?" or "What's been stressing you out the most lately?" help both people understand how much the other person is holding.

Some jobs aren't even obvious, like being the one who helps each other feel better or remembers all the little things, like bills or birthdays. When these efforts are recognized and thanked, they make both people feel important. This makes you feel better emotionally and lowers your anger.

Teamwork is also based on knowing your role. Partners start to ask, "How can we make this feel more fair?" or "Can we switch tasks for a while?" instead of saying, "That's your job." These talks show that you are willing to change and care. They make both people feel like they are on the same team, not like they are competing and trying to keep score. Say "thank you" for the little things. Gratitude should be shared regularly, even for everyday tasks. A simple "Thanks for cooking tonight" or "I noticed you folded my laundry" makes someone feel seen and appreciated.

It's simple to judge things we don't know. "They're overreacting" might be the first thing that comes to mind when a partner gets upset over something small. It could look like they don't care if they pull away instead of talking. People often act out of pain from the past, stress that they don't want to show, or unmet needs. As soon as a partner judges too quickly, they close off mental safety. But when they stop judging and start being curious then, they connect more deeply.

Instead of thinking, "They never listen to me," someone might think, "I wonder if they're busy or distracted right now." The thought of that makes me more patient. Another thought that might be more helpful than "They're just lazy" is "Maybe they're not motivated because they're stressed out or burned out." Discussions become calmer when people have these softer thoughts. They want to be cared for instead of criticized.

Instead of making conclusions, it is helpful to ask open-ended questions. "Why are you acting that way?" is not as good of a question as "Can you help me understand what's going on?" The first one makes you want to connect. The second one makes space. Being kind with your words changes everything.

When couples stop judging each other and start knowing each other, they are often surprised. They start to see more of each other. They find out about fears, hopes, and inner struggles they didn't know they had. These findings help people understand each other better and strengthen the bond between them.

Respect each other's emotional pace. Not everyone processes feelings at the same speed. Give your partner the time they need to open up. Pressuring someone to talk before they're ready makes them shut down more.

Making a relationship a culture of care isn't about keeping bad feelings from coming up. It's about getting the tools you need to handle them with style. The relationship gets stronger every time both people try to listen better, understand each other better, and react with more kindness. Partners believe each other, share, and grow as a couple.

Couples should understand and care for each other. It changes times of pain into chances to get better. It makes everyday life more loving. When a partner makes them feel known, cared for, and fully understood, they become their best selves. They build a life together that isn't just based on love but also on kindness, care, and emotional depth.

Chapter 5:
Supporting Each Other's Aspirations and Professional Growth

Ambition is a powerful thing. It drives us to reach for bigger goals to push ourselves to achieve what others might think is impossible. But while ambition gives us purpose and direction, it's important to remember that strong relationships are just as valuable. Having someone who supports and believes in you makes the journey toward your dreams much more meaningful. When both partners have big dreams, it sometimes feels like a struggle to balance those personal goals with shared aspirations.

In the beginning, it might feel like a perfect balance, two people, each working toward their own career, dreams, and passions. But as time goes on, things become more complicated. Both partners are working hard to build something, and it sometimes feels like there's not enough time or energy left to nurture the relationship. Balancing your personal life along with your dreams is challenging, but it's not impossible. When couples figure out how to support each other while still growing individually, they achieve great things together.

I'm sharing a few scenarios and practical tips for couples with big ambitions on how to support each other while keeping their own goals intact. These strategies will help you maintain a loving, fulfilling partnership while also pursuing personal and shared dreams:

- The foundation of any strong relationship is communication. If both partners have big ambitions, it's important to talk about them openly. Share your dreams and aspirations with each other, even the small, vulnerable ones. Let your partner know what your goals are and ask about theirs. When both partners understand each other's desires, it becomes easier to find ways to support one another without stepping on each other's toes.

- While it's important to maintain your own goals, it's equally important to have shared goals. Set a few goals together that both of you are excited about. It could be something simple, like saving for a trip or buying a house, or something bigger, like working together on a project. Having something to work toward as a couple helps you stay connected and gives both partners something to look forward to together.

- Ambition requires focus, and sometimes, that focus means needing time and space to work on personal goals. This doesn't mean a lack of love or commitment, but rather an understanding that both people need time to pursue their own passions. It's fine for one person to spend a few late nights working on a project while the other relaxes or pursues their own interests. Give each other the space to grow while knowing that it's only temporary.

- No victory is too small to celebrate. Whether it's getting a new job, finishing a big project, or hitting a milestone, take the time to recognize and celebrate each other's successes. It strengthens the bond between you both, and it shows that you're genuinely rooting for each other. Don't let your ambitions drive a wedge between you; instead, let them bring you closer as you cheer each other on.

- Ambition sometimes leads to busy schedules, but it's essential to make time for the relationship. Regularly scheduled date nights, even if it's just a walk together or cooking dinner at home. These moments are an opportunity to reconnect, talk about your goals, and remind each other that the relationship matters, too. Life gets hectic, but making time for each other is a choice that shows you're committed to the relationship.

- Learn to support without always solving. When your partner faces a setback or challenge, resist the urge to immediately jump in with solutions. Sometimes, they just need to be heard and reassured. Being a supportive partner doesn't always mean fixing things; it often means listening, validating their feelings, and being a calming presence. Your emotional availability during tough times deepens your bond and shows that you're a true partner through both wins and losses.

- While ambition drives you toward personal success, never lose sight of the fact that your partner is also a big part of your journey. The most successful relationships are the ones where both partners work toward their dreams, but never at the expense of the relationship itself. Always check in with each other to make sure both your individual dreams and shared goals are aligned, and make sure you're both happy in the relationship.

Balancing ambition and a strong relationship isn't always easy, but it's definitely possible. When both partners are driven by personal goals, there's a natural tendency to want to work harder, achieve more, and sometimes even compete with each other. However, instead of seeing each other's ambitions as a threat, remember that you're on the same team and not rivals. One person's success is both of your successes. Adopting this perspective will bring you closer.

By being open, supportive, and respectful, couples create an environment where both individuals are encouraged to pursue their dreams while also nurturing the relationship. Supporting each other's goals doesn't mean giving up on your own, and it certainly doesn't mean sacrificing your happiness. It's about finding a balance where both partners grow individually and together, side by side.

Remember, it's not about one person's success overshadowing the other's; it's about both partners lifting each other up and growing together. The journey toward your personal and shared goals is much more enjoyable when you're not alone. The real reward isn't just achieving your personal dreams but doing so with someone who understands and shares your vision. Ambition and love don't have to be separate; they work together in harmony, making the whole experience better.

At the end of the day, both ambition and love are powerful forces. They drive us, inspire us, and push us toward becoming better versions of ourselves. But it's when we learn to balance them, when we learn to support each other without losing sight of our own dreams, that we truly find success, not just in our ambitions, but in our relationships, too.

Being in a relationship means you have someone by your side who lifts you up, encourages you, and helps you get through tough times. But being a supportive partner doesn't mean giving up your own dreams or personal success. Instead, it's about helping each other achieve your goals, offering encouragement when things get hard, and finding ways to balance both your individual dreams and the relationship itself.

There's a common misconception that if you want to be a supportive partner, you have to put your own aspirations aside for the sake of the relationship, and that is not true. Support isn't about sacrificing your success; it's about creating a partnership where both people thrive. Each person should have the freedom to chase their dreams and grow in their own way while still being there for each other through the ups and downs.

Being there for your partner during times of success and failure is one of the most meaningful things you should do in a relationship. It's about recognizing that each person's goals matter and that it's okay to experience both wins and losses together. When both partners support each other, they don't just help each other succeed, but they also help each other get back on track after setbacks, too.

The key is to find ways to support your partner without losing sight of your own path. In any relationship, there's a natural tendency to want to succeed. However, it's important to remember that one person's success doesn't take away from the others. Encouraging each other without comparing achievements or competing with one another is important. A supportive partner is genuinely happy for the other person's success, knowing that it doesn't take anything away from their own achievements. When your partner wins, celebrate with them, and when you succeed, expect the same in return.

Success is not always linear. Sometimes, setbacks and failures are a part of the journey. A supportive partner understands that and stands by their loved one during tough times. It's easy to feel discouraged when things aren't going well, but knowing that your partner is there to help you bounce back makes all the difference. Offer words of encouragement, listen without judgment, and remind each other that setbacks are only temporary. A little support goes a long way when things feel tough.

One of the most important ways to support each other is to communicate openly and honestly. Therefore, you should talk about your goals, your dreams, and your challenges with each other. Let your partner know when you need help or when you're struggling. This creates a safe space where both of you will be vulnerable without feeling weak or misunderstood. It's okay to admit that you need support; in fact, it makes the bond even stronger. Be a good listener, offer advice when needed, and know when to just be there to offer comfort.

When you both have personal goals, it's important to respect each other's time and boundaries. Support doesn't mean you're always available to drop everything for your partner. Instead, it's about understanding when your partner needs time to focus on their work or personal goals. Establishing clear boundaries, whether it's about work, social time, or quiet time, helps you both maintain your personal life while being a supportive partner. It's okay to give each other space to pursue your dreams.

Moreover, offering support means helping out in practical ways. If your partner is working toward a big goal, whether it's advancing in their career, finishing a degree, or starting a new business, practical help is invaluable. This could be as simple as making dinner while they work late or taking on some household responsibilities when they're overwhelmed. Small gestures of support make a big difference and allow your partner to focus on what's important without feeling drained by the day-to-day tasks.

While being supportive of your partner's ambitions is important, it's just as important to keep pursuing your own goals. A healthy relationship allows both people to grow individually while also growing together. Make sure you're setting aside time for your own passions and pursuits. Whether it's advancing in your career, learning something new, or simply having time for yourself, make sure you're nurturing your own ambitions. When both partners are working toward their personal goals, they each bring energy and inspiration into the relationship, which makes it even stronger.

Sometimes, life doesn't go according to plan. You might not achieve your goals as quickly as you hoped, or your partner might face a setback. It's important to be patient with each other during these times. Understand that both of you are doing your best, and there will be highs and lows in any journey. Offering patience and understanding when things don't go as planned shows that you are in it together for the long haul.

As both of you pursue your goals, there will be new opportunities to learn from each other. Maybe one partner learns something new that benefits the other, or perhaps one person's success will inspire the other to dream bigger. A supportive partner helps their loved one grow and evolve, and the relationship grows stronger when both people are encouraged to keep learning and expanding.

Careers are a big part of life. They bring excitement, purpose, and personal fulfillment, but they also come with challenges. Long hours, frequent deadlines, and constant stress take a toll, not just on you but also on your relationship. For couples, balancing professional growth with a strong, loving partnership is tricky. Yet, when both partners face these obstacles together, it makes the relationship even stronger.

Long work hours are one of the most common career challenges that many people face. It's easy to get caught up in the hustle of work, especially when you're passionate about your job or working towards a big promotion. However, when one or both partners are working long hours, it strains the time spent together. This lack of time leads to feelings of neglect, frustration, and sometimes even resentment. But it doesn't have to break the relationship.

A supportive partner understands that sometimes work requires extra time, and instead of being upset, they find ways to support the other person's professional goals. This could mean adjusting schedules to create quality time together or simply offering emotional support during busy periods. A relationship that's built on mutual understanding, weather the challenges of long hours without affecting the love between the partners.

Another challenge is frequent travel. Jobs that require travel often leave one partner feeling lonely or disconnected. Traveling for work might mean that your partner is away for days or even weeks at a time. This is tough on any relationship. Missing each other leads to feelings of sadness, frustration, or even doubt. But when couples work together to manage this time apart, they stay connected despite the distance.

Here are five simple things couples should do to stay connected during times of distance:

- A quick "good morning" or "thinking of you" message brightens your partner's day and helps you feel close, even when you're far apart.
- Even a short conversation at the end of the day makes a big difference in feeling emotionally connected.
- Send a photo of your meal, a funny meme, or a quick update about your day. It will make your partner feel included in your life.
- Make plans for a date, a weekend trip, or even a cozy night in when you're back. Having something to look forward to makes the time apart easier.

- A handwritten note tucked in a bag, a surprise delivery, or a kind email is a sweet reminder of your love and effort.

These small gestures may seem simple, but they build a strong emotional bridge across the distance. With a little effort and care, love grows even when miles apart.

In some cases, the stress from work itself is overwhelming. Deadlines, high expectations, and difficult situations at work cause tension, frustration, and burnout. When one partner is under stress, it spills over into the relationship. This is where partnership is important and needed. A strong partnership means being there to listen, offering a safe space for venting, and providing emotional support when things get tough. Even if you don't have the solution to your partner's work problems, showing that you're there for them is incredibly comforting.

It's also important for couples to be mindful of how stress is managed in the relationship. If one partner is constantly stressed, it affects the atmosphere at home. It's helpful to have discussions about how both partners deal with stress and work out ways to support each other during those times. For example, one person might prefer to talk things through, while the other might need time alone to decompress. Understanding these preferences and respecting each other's coping methods will help maintain a peaceful balance at home.

Even with all the challenges that careers bring, working together as a team allows couples to work through these obstacles while maintaining a loving and fulfilling relationship. It's about finding ways to prioritize the partnership, even when work demands so much of your time and energy. Whether it's taking turns handling responsibilities at home, communicating about your needs, or making time for each other, the effort you put into maintaining your bond is worth it.

By working together, couples turn professional challenges into opportunities to grow as a team. For instance, when one partner faces a difficult project or a big career change, it is a chance for both partners to come together and problem-solve. Rather than letting these challenges create distance, they become moments where the relationship is strengthened. Being there for each other through the tough times not only helps your partner but also helps you build resilience as a couple.

Career challenges are an unavoidable part of life, but they don't have to get in the way of a fulfilling relationship. In fact, facing them together makes the connection between partners even deeper. Couples who support each other through stress show that love and teamwork overcome even the most difficult obstacles. When both partners work toward maintaining a balance between their professional goals and their relationship, the result is a strong, loving partnership that survives in any storm.

The bond that comes from facing career challenges together lasts a lifetime. It's built on trust, communication, and a shared sense of purpose. By understanding each other's goals and being there to support them, both partners experience professional growth without sacrificing their relationship. The most successful couples are the ones who learn how to adapt, communicate, and find creative solutions to challenges. They see obstacles as something to tackle together, not as something that will tear them apart.

Ultimately, a strong relationship isn't about avoiding challenges but about facing them together. The effort you put into your relationship when career challenges arise shows the depth of your commitment.

Chapter 6:
Surviving Work-Related
Long-Distance Relationships

There are hundreds or millions of people who are working far away from their homes to earn a living. Similarly, some of them are couples who have to live in different cities or countries because of their jobs. They still love each other and want to be together, but it's hard for them to be apart. The problem isn't just that they live far apart; they also miss each other, feel lonely, and try to stay close even when they can't be together.

People get involved in long-distance relationships because of the career or better future they pursue; however, they do not understand the outcomes of being distant in their relationship. Getting a new job in a different city, being sent to war, traveling for business all the time, or signing a long-term contract to work abroad put even the strongest relationships to the test. There may still be love, but the ways of showing it are very different.

The first thing most couples notice is the silence. It is not the silence of calmness but it's something else. The kind of silence that starts before dinner, while you're watching TV, or while you're in bed by yourself. It starts to feel heavy not having any physical touch and sharing the same roof. People not only miss hearing someone's voice. It's about missing the whole person's presence—the little things they do, the things or memories you have been sharing, and the emotional connection.

Over time, emotional disconnection becomes a real risk. Without physical closeness, it's harder to read each other's moods, sense when something's wrong, or offer comfort in real-time. Communication becomes limited to phone calls, texts, or video calls. Though it is helpful to stay connected a bit, still technology cannot replace the subtle emotional support of simply being in the same room.

People in long-distance situations often begin to feel like they're living separate lives. One person might be adjusting to a new environment, new coworkers, different routines, and unfamiliar surroundings, while the other continues on with their life at home. Therefore, these two different kinds of feelings create emotional gaps. The couple is still connected, but that connection starts to stretch thin.

Then, feelings of insecurity start to enter in mind, and thoughts creep in, like "Do they still miss me?" "What if they're changing, and I'm not part of it?" "What if someone else catches their attention?" These questions are normal, but they hurt and lead to fear, jealousy, and anger. If you will not talk about these feelings with your partner then they will damage trust.

Therefore, simple things make you feel jealous. Such as a photo with new friends, a missed call, or a story about a coworker that seems just a little too friendly. The mind makes up threats even when there are not any actual situation. Staying far away makes you question yourself. Therefore, if you don't get reassurance, then these feelings become permanent and may cause you to have further issues.

Miscommunication adds another layer of difficulty. A short text may be misunderstood. A missed goodnight call might feel like rejection. One partner could be tired from work, while the other is wide awake and craving connection. Different time zones or busy work schedules make it hard to find time for each other. Even small misunderstandings grow into bigger arguments when there's no physical way to reconnect quickly.

There's also the internal conflict that comes with trying to balance love and ambition. The person who left for work might feel guilty for causing the separation, even if it was for the right reasons. The one who stayed behind might feel guilty for struggling, for needing more attention, and for not being supportive. This push and pull of emotions makes everything feel more intense.

The truth is that missing someone every day hurts. It's not a weakness; it's just part of being human. Also, wanting a hug, having breakfast together, or holding hands after a tough day isn't about being needy. It's about wanting closeness. And when that need isn't met, no matter how much effort goes into messages or video chats, the relationship feels weak. If there were problems in the relationship before the distance started, they usually get worse. Without spending time together, it's harder to fix issues. A conversation that would've taken ten minutes in person can turn into days of tension over text. There's no quick forgiveness with a hug, no easy way to say 'I'm sorry' in person. Distance makes every feeling stronger.

Some couples avoid talking about the tough things. They might say, 'Everything's fine,' when it's not. They might hide their feelings to avoid stressing their partner. But ignoring the pain delays healing. Unspoken feelings don't go away; they build up and can turn into anger, disinterest, or distance.

Even with all these challenges, long-distance relationships don't have to end in heartbreak. Many couples have become stronger than before. It takes effort, but it's possible. The key? Trust, communication, and a shared commitment.

I'm sharing five simple and strong tips to make your long-distance relationships easier:

- Build your relationship on trust because it is the most important part of a long-distance relationship. Without it, every missed message or new name leads to doubt and stress. Trust doesn't mean ignoring problems, but it means believing in your partner and the bond you share. Even when worries come up, trust means choosing to believe in each other instead of giving in to fear. A strong sense of trust gives both people peace of mind and helps the relationship feel safe, even from far away.

- Go deeper with your communication because talking about your day is good, but real closeness comes from sharing feelings. Saying things like "I feel lonely," "I miss you," or "This is really hard for me" creates an honest and open connection. It's important to have a space where both people speak freely without any judgments. These deeper talks help you understand each other better and feel emotionally close, even when you're not physically together.

- Create routines that keep you connected; little routines go a long way in keeping the bond strong. Plan regular times to video chat, watch the same movie while on call, or send each other playlists or journal updates. These habits may seem small, but they help create shared experiences and moments that feel special. They remind both people that love is still present, even though a screen.

- Have a plan for the future; it's easier to stay strong when there's a goal to work toward. Whether it's the next visit or a long-term plan to live together, having something to look forward to gives hope. Without a clear idea of when the distance will end, the relationship starts to feel uncertain or draining. But a plan, even if it's far off, gives both people a sense of direction and reminds them that the distance is only temporary.

- Make each other part of everyday life even when you're far apart. There are many ways to stay involved in each other's daily routines. Send a photo of your lunch, record a quick voice note, or leave a sweet message. These small acts show love, effort, and thoughtfulness. Doing such things conveys a message, "I care about you," even without saying a word. Over time, these little moments help build a feeling of closeness that keeps the relationship strong.

At the end of the day, long-distance relationships created by work are a test of patience, effort, and emotional strength. They need daily efforts to stay connected, be honest, and trust each other. Distance might separate two people, but it doesn't have to separate their hearts.

Love doesn't disappear just because two people are far apart; it changes shape. It asks for new ways to be expressed. When someone can't be there to hold a hand or share a quiet evening together, they must build bridges to stay close, bridges made from communication, creativity, and care. Many couples in long-distance relationships ask this same question, "how can we keep the spark alive when we're so far apart?" The answer lies in finding fresh ways to stay emotionally and romantically connected. It starts with effort, intentional, consistent effort from both people.

One of the easiest ways to stay close is by being creative with how you communicate. It doesn't always have to be serious talks. Sometimes, the small moments matter the most. Watching the same show and texting reactions. Sending funny memes to make each other laugh. Leaving voice notes with sleepy greetings or quick check-ins. These little things remind each other that you are thinking of them.

Video dates are another great way to feel together, even when apart. Dressing up for a virtual dinner, lighting candles, and eating together over a video call bring back some of the normalcy of in-person dates. Others play online games, do trivia nights, or use apps that let them take personality quizzes together. It's not about the activity but it's about sharing time and attention. There's also something deeply romantic about going old school. Sending handwritten letters or small surprise gifts means more than anything typed on a screen. A simple note tucked into a mailed package or a care box filled with favorites, like snacks, books, or photos, brings real joy.

Planning surprise visits, when possible, also makes the long distance quite fun. Even if it's just for a weekend, the energy and excitement leading up to seeing each other in person creates something to look forward to. The build-up of anticipation and the relief of physical presence, even if short, recharges emotional batteries. After the visit ends, the memories give something sweet to hold onto until the next time.

Technology has become a powerful ally for long-distance couples. There are apps designed specifically for relationships that let partners share calendars, send quick love notes, and track shared goals. Some help with managing different time zones, reminding both people when it's a good time to call. Others allow for joint journals, shared to-do lists, or virtual date ideas.

Having a shared calendar helps coordinate schedules. It becomes easier to plan weekly video calls or find windows of time to talk without interruptions. Even blocking out 30 minutes once a week as "together time" builds routine and trust. It shows both people are making space for the relationship in their busy lives. Routine is the key. Without it, everything starts to feel uncertain. Building a rhythm helps create emotional safety. Whether it's "Sunday night check-ins" or "Wednesday movie nights," setting regular touchpoints gives both partners something to count on. A routine doesn't make things boring; it makes them reliable.

But the connection isn't just about scheduling calls or sending cute messages. It's also about speaking the kind of language that builds intimacy. Affirming words like "I'm proud of you," "I miss you," and "Thank you for making time for us" go a long way. These phrases, when spoken often and sincerely, help close the emotional distance. They fill in the gaps that physical touch usually bridges.

Checking in emotionally is another powerful habit. Not just "How was your day?" but questions like, "How are you really feeling today?" or "Is there anything you need from me right now?" These deeper conversations remind each person they're seen and valued, not just as a partner, but as a whole person. Celebrating small milestones is just as important. Whether it's one week, one month, or one year apart, every moment survived together deserves recognition.

For many, what matters most isn't grand gestures; it's the consistency. A good morning message, a reminder to eat lunch, a nighttime call before going to bed even if it's short, these routines build security. It is a way to show that they are still a part of your everyday life. When these things are missing, the distance starts to feel heavier, but when they're present, love feels active. Of course, not every day is perfect. There are days when work is stressful, time zones don't align, or emotions run high. That's when grace and patience are most needed. Understanding that sometimes one person might need space or that missed calls aren't signs of disinterest helps reduce unnecessary tension.

It's also helpful to talk about the hard stuff before it becomes a problem. Discussing expectations, boundaries, and emotional needs upfront avoids misunderstandings. For example, agreeing on how often to talk, how to handle missed check-ins, or how to deal with jealousy sets a healthy foundation.

And perhaps most importantly, couples must keep reminding each other why they're choosing to stay connected. Revisiting shared goals, dreams for the future, and the vision for life after the distance ends reignites motivation. It turns the separation into something with purpose, not just a pause, but a part of the story.

Some couples even use their time apart to grow individually. They pick up hobbies, read new books, or work on personal goals. Then, they share their growth with each other. It gives them more to talk about, and it reminds them that their love supports who they're becoming, not just who they've been.

In a long-distance relationship, there are many distractions that do not let you stay close to your partner. It takes effort and love to maintain a healthy relationship. When people try to stay connected with their partner even after living far away, the spark stays alive in their relationship. Love isn't about living nearby; it's about being there for each other. When two people really want to stay together, their presence is felt even from far away because of their efforts in the relationship.

Chapter 7:
Parenting in the Pursuit of Success

Sometimes, parents are so busy that they forget to slow down in their lives. They wake up early, rush to work, sit in long meetings, or run their own businesses. They want to do well to earn more money and be proud of their jobs, which is also not a bad thing. Working hard helps pay for food, clothes, and a nice home. Therefore, the children at home may feel lonely and unwelcome. They may feel like they are waiting all the time for a hug, for a dinner together, or just for someone to listen. While parents are chasing big dreams, their children are quietly missing them at home.

Parents who work hard to succeed in their jobs often feel empty inside. They want to do well at work and reach their goals. But they also want to be good parents who spend time with their kids, show love, and pay attention to them. The problem is that they have very limited time to enjoy, so when they have to choose to do something, something usually gets left behind. A lot of the time, it's the time parents spend really connecting with their children that starts to disappear.

Many parents don't mean to be distant; they are simply busy. Sometimes, work takes longer than planned. Meetings run late, travel plans are busy, and there are many deadlines to meet. However, their children don't even have an idea what their parents are facing. To a child, when a parent isn't there, it might not feel like the parent is busy with work; it might feel like the parent doesn't care. The child might think, "Mom doesn't love me," or "Dad is always too busy to spend time with me." Even though the parent is working hard to help the family, the child might still feel alone or like they are not important. This emotional distance hurts children more than many parents know. It's not just about being in the same room with them; It's about being there for them emotionally, too.

A person might be home, but if they are too tired, busy, or stressed, they might not be able to really connect with their children. When a parent isn't emotionally available, it hurts a child's feelings deeply, and those feelings stay with them for a long time. Basically, it's the communication gap that comes between parents and children.

Children who grow up with parents who are not emotionally available may feel like they are not good enough for their parents. They might believe they need to work hard to get love or attention from others. Some children might act out in school or at home because they want people to notice them. Other children might become quiet and keep their feelings inside because they think no one will care about their feelings. This kind of hurt does not go away quickly. It stays with them as they grow up and affects how they feel about themselves, how they connect with others, and even their mental health.

Even parents who love their children still fall into this problem. The wish to be successful is strong, especially when society values hard work and ambition. But when the price of success is the happiness and emotional health of a child, then parents need to change their ways of approaching things. It's not always easy, but trying to show love and support for your child, both in person and emotionally, can make a big difference.

Sometimes, the parent who stays at home feels overwhelmed, whether it is the mother or the father. They might have to do all the parenting and manage everything in the house by themselves. This causes stress, anger, or frustration, which might end up being directed at the children. When one parent feels like they are doing everything alone and the other is always busy, the family starts to break down because of the pressure.

Therefore, to stop this from happening, both parents need to work together as a team. Talking to each other is very important. Even if one parent is often away, they must have open and honest talks about how the family is doing, what the children need, and how they need to share the responsibilities more fairly. When parents respect and support each other, children feel safe and loved even when things are hard. That's why it's so important to find small but special ways to stay connected. A bedtime story, a quick video call during lunch break, or even a short message before a big school test, these little things show children that they are noticed and important.

I have a close friend who shared her story with me, one that deeply touched me because it showed how hard it is to balance love, work, and family. Joseph and Nadhia had been married for sixteen years. Their journey as a couple and parents had its challenges, especially since Nadhia worked as a compliance officer at a major bank. Her job required long hours, frequent travel, and late-night work, which sometimes made it hard for the family to stay connected. Joseph often found himself handling most of the parenting and household responsibilities, especially when Nadhia was away.

Moreover, their son, Naijoel, really missed his mom when she was not around. He had a hard time with the change in his daily routine, and because of this, Joseph had to do more. He didn't only have a father's responsibilities; he also needed to be a strong and dependable person in Naijoel's life. It was not always easy for him. The couple came from different cultures as Nadhia is Angolan, and Joseph is American. Sometimes, this caused misunderstandings between them. Their ways of parenting and talking to each other were influenced by their cultures, which made things a bit more complicated. But over time, they learned to accept these differences, and they began to see them as strengths that helped them become closer and grow together.

Joseph had his own struggles because he grew up without a father, so he didn't have anyone to show him how to be a good dad. Sometimes, when Naijoel needed to learn discipline, Joseph would yell at him. He thought that was the best way to teach him a lesson. But over time, Joseph saw that yelling didn't really help, and it wasn't the kind of father he wanted to be. With prayer, support from Nadhia, and his strong faith, Joseph began to change. He started working on being more patient and understanding with his son. Despite all these challenges, Joseph and Nadhia found ways to make their relationship and family stronger. They made intentional changes to improve their marriage and parenting.

Even when Nadhia was away, they all stayed close and connected. She would call Naijoel and send him voice messages so he could still hear her voice and feel her love. When she came back home, they made sure to spend special time together as a family. They turned off phones, put away distractions, and focused on each other. They gave their full attention, showing that family time was important. Their faith community also helped them a lot. Joseph's mother-in-law also played an important role in between, especially when Nadhia had to travel. She helped take care of Naijoel and made sure he felt safe and loved. Joseph also took on more jobs at home. He made sure that Naijoel had a steady routine every day. Both parents worked together to mix their cultures. They wanted Naijoel to feel proud of being both Angolan and American, and to understand and enjoy both parts of his background.

Faith was at the center of their family life. They made time each day to read the Bible and pray together. Their faith guided them in their decisions and helped them find peace during tough times. They also put effort into their marriage. They would reflect on what they loved about each other and the areas they needed to improve. They made sure to plan together, aligning their goals and responsibilities despite their busy lives.

Even though they had made a lot of progress, Joseph and Nadhia knew there was still more work to do. They wanted to make sure that family time stayed important, even with Nadhia's busy job. They were trying to set better limits at work for her, so she could have a healthier balance between her job and her time with family. They also wanted to bring their two cultures together more smoothly, so that Naijoel could feel proud of both his Angolan and American roots. Talking openly and honestly was very important for them. They worked hard to keep their communication strong, so they could continue growing as a family. Even though Joseph grew up without a father, his faith helped him. He believed that God was leading him and teaching him how to be the husband and father his family needed. He knew he still had a lot to learn, but he trusted that God was helping him every step of the way.

Therefore, staying connected as a couple and as a family is one of the most important ways to protect relationships during such situations. Even when a parent is far from home because of work, there are small, powerful ways to stay present. A video call before bedtime, a kind message during the day, or a photo shared from a trip makes a big difference in a child's heart. These gestures tell the child, "You matter to me," and that message is needed just as much as food or shelter. Physical absence is difficult, but emotional absence cuts deeper. Children don't always say when they're feeling lonely or ignored, but they feel it, and it shows up in their behavior, self-esteem, or ability to trust.

That's why it is so important for parents to work together as a team. An extended family might be a big help when parents are trying to find balance in their busy lives. Family members, such as uncles, aunts, and grandparents, or else closest family friends give support in multiple ways. They might pick up a child from school, help cook a meal, or just listen when things feel hard, similarly, as it happens in Nadhia's story.

Moreover, asking for help is not a sign of weakness; it actually shows strength and wisdom. It takes courage to say, "I can't do this alone." Having a good support system doesn't mean that parents are doing less. It simply means that others are helping when life gets stressful. This kind of help doesn't take the place of a parent, but it fills in the spaces when parents are tired or busy. It also teaches children that love comes from many people and not just from mom or dad.

Being emotionally present is not always easy. After a long day at work, a parent might feel tired, stressed, or not in the mood to talk. It's easy to get distracted or lose patience. But small and thoughtful choices make a big difference. Here are some simple ways to be emotionally present:

- Turn off your phone during family time. When you turn off your phone at dinner or during conversations, it shows your child that they are more important than any calls or messages. It helps you focus fully on them and the moment you share together.

- Make eye contact when your child speaks. Eye contact is a powerful way to show your child that you are paying attention. It makes them feel heard and respected, which is important to building emotional trust.

- Listen without interrupting and let your child express their thoughts completely before responding. When you allow them to speak freely, it helps them feel understood and valued.

- Spend a few minutes at bedtime to talk or pray together. Bedtime is a special time to connect. Whether you read stories, talk about the day, or say a prayer together, it creates a peaceful ending to their day and strengthens your emotional bond.

- Ask how their day was and really listen. Take the time to ask your child about their day, showing real interest in their feelings and experiences. This lets them know their thoughts and emotions matter to you.

- Give a hug, a smile, or a kind word. Simple gestures like hugs, smiles, or telling them you love them help your child feel safe and cared for. Physical touch and kind words make a big difference in how emotionally supported they feel.

- Be patient when they are upset. When your child is frustrated or upset, try to stay calm and patient. Help them work through their emotions without rushing them. Let them know it's okay to feel what they're feeling and that you're there for them.

These things are really very small actions, but they create a strong emotional connection and help your child feel safe and loved. Remember, it's not about being perfect; it's about showing up with love and intention, even in small ways.

Parenting is not only about teaching children what is right or wrong. It is also about growing as adults. Parents need to learn how to listen better, be more patient, and understand their children's feelings. No parent is perfect, and no one gets everything right all the time. But it's important to be willing to think about how things went, say sorry when needed, and try again. This helps build trust not just with children, but also between parents. What makes a family strong is not being perfect, but being consistent, kind, and believing that every person in the family is important. When parents show these qualities, it creates a loving and supportive family where everyone feels valued.

Moreover, children don't need perfect parents. They need present ones, parents who show up, listen, and keep trying, even when they feel tired or unsure. The truth is, parenting doesn't come with a guide. Every child is different, and so is every season of life. What worked last year may not work today, but that's okay. The most important thing is to keep showing up with love and the willingness to learn. When a child sees a parent making an effort, apologizing when they're wrong, learning to communicate better, or just being there even in silence, it teaches them that love grows through effort.

Touch matters too, like a gentle pat on the back, a cuddle on the couch, or a kiss on the forehead. These small actions may only take a few seconds, but they carry deep meaning. Physical affection, along with saying "I love you," helps children understand that they are important, not just for what they do, but for who they are. In a world that often tells people they need to do more, a loving home says, "You are enough."

Over time, these constant acts of love build the child's sense of security. When life gets difficult, and it will, they will turn back to this love. It's what keeps them feeling safe when everything else feels uncertain. It teaches them how to care for others, speak kindly, and stay strong when things are hard. This is the gift parents give every day, not through being perfect, but by being present.

Chapter 8:
God as the Foundation of Your Relationship

Faith makes a relationship stronger because it helps both people feel safe and steady, even during hard times. Relationships are not always easy; there are happy moments, but there are also struggles and challenges. When two people believe in the same things, especially spiritually, they feel closer and more connected. Their faith gives them hope and guidance when life gets tough. It helps them solve problems together as a team instead of facing everything alone. Faith becomes something they trust and depend on. I want to share the story of a close friend named Carl. His journey through love, marriage, and faith taught me a lot, and I believe it will speak to others as well.

Carl had been married four times, but it wasn't until the fourth marriage that he finally understood what real love, marriage, and a God-centered partnership should be like. His first marriage happened when he was only 18; he was too young at the time. Carl believed he was ready, but the truth was, he didn't even know who he was yet. He didn't understand how to love someone or lead in a relationship. That marriage didn't last, and when it ended, Carl carried the hurt with him into the next part of his life.

Carl's second marriage was based on revenge. He wasn't taking time to heal; he was reacting out of pain. He didn't ask God for guidance. Instead, he rushed into the relationship, trying to prove something, maybe to others, or maybe just to himself, but revenge can't build a healthy home. It breaks things before they even begin to happen. Moreover, his third marriage was all about money. Carl thought that having financial security and success would make him feel whole, but it didn't. That relationship looked good on the outside, but it was empty on the inside, like a nicely wrapped gift with nothing in it. He had someone by his side, but he didn't feel peaceful. He had a partner, but their life together had no real meaning.

Through all of this, Carl was hiding his true feelings, struggles, or identity from others. He grew up in a Christian home. He went to church four times a week. He sang lead in the choir and took part in every church play. He knew the Bible well and could quote verses easily, but he wasn't living by them. As Carl got older, he didn't carry those Christian values into his adult life. Somewhere along the way, he walked away from the strong foundation his stepmother had given him. He tried to build his life on his own terms. He didn't let the Holy Spirit guide him. He thought he could handle everything by himself. But the truth was, he couldn't.

Then, Carl went to Angola, Africa, and by the time Carl reached there for work, he had completely written off marriage. He told himself he was done trying. But in his spirit, he felt a quiet voice say, "There's something special for you here." He didn't understand it at the time, but now he knows that "something special" was Aline.

At first, Carl didn't want to try again. He had already been through three failed marriages, and he didn't want to go through the pain again, but Aline was different. She had a calm strength and a clear sense of direction. Most importantly, she put God first in everything she did, which made Carl stop and think about her. He wasn't used to being with a woman who truly lived by Christian values. Aline didn't just care about Carl as a person; she cared about building a healthy relationship with him, one that honored God. That was new for him, and it made him see things differently.

Still, it wasn't always easy. There were times when Carl felt like giving up again, just like he had before. It was hard to break old habits. Walking away had always been easier than working through the pain, but this time was different because he stayed. He chose to pray instead of run. He stopped letting fear control him and started letting the Holy Spirit guide him. And because of that, everything began to change for the better.

Carl and Aline have now been married for almost 17 years. God has been with them every step of the way. He shaped them, held them together, and turned their marriage into a powerful example of His love and faithfulness. Through Aline, Carl discovered that marriage isn't just about being happy; it's about being spiritually active. It's not about following your own plans, but surrendering to God's. It is about facing tough times with faith and humility, not pride or selfishness. Carl is still growing and learning, but now, he's not walking this path by himself. God has brought healing to his life. He has taken Carl's broken story and turned it into something good. Every day, Carl thanks God for never giving up on him, even during the times when Carl had given up on himself.

Carl's story is a reminder that it's never too late to change, to grow, or to start again. His past was full of mistakes, but his future became evidence of grace, healing, and the power of a God who restores. Through love, faith, and a willingness to let go of pride, Carl found peace, not just in marriage, but in himself. His journey isn't over, but now he walks it with purpose, guided by the one who never left his side.

Moreover, when couples believe in the same spiritual values, they feel more connected to each other. They are able to understand each other in a deeper and more meaningful way. Faith is not only something they speak about during prayer. It becomes part of their daily lives and guides how they live each day. Their faith shows in the way they speak to each other, in the choices they make, and in the things they do. When both people believe in being kind, forgiving, and honest, their relationship becomes calm, caring, and full of love. These values are not just thoughts or words; they are daily habits that shape how each person treats the other.

Having a spiritual connection is different from liking the same movies, music, or hobbies. It goes much deeper than enjoying the same activities. A spiritual connection means that two people see the world in a similar way. They share the same beliefs about what is most important in life. This shared view creates a strong emotional and spiritual bond between them. It helps them stay close not only during happy times, but also when they are going through pain, fear, or hard situations. When a couple prays together or talks about their faith, they build a strong and lasting connection that keeps them united.

Faith also helps bring stability to a relationship because it becomes part of a couple's daily life. When two people include faith in their daily routine, they create stable and peaceful ways to deal with life. They might pray before eating and sleeping, attend church services together, or read the holy scriptures side by side. These small actions help bring a sense of calm and order to their lives. These moments remind the couple that they are part of something greater than just themselves. They know they are not facing life alone. This gives comfort to their hearts and minds. Even when life feels hard or confusing, their faith gives them hope, guidance, and a clear path to follow.

Moreover, when a couple keeps God at the center of their relationship, it helps them feel more united. It reminds both people that their love has a special and higher purpose. They are not just loving each other to feel happy. They are also loving each other to show respect and honor to God. This helps them stay kind and humble. It helps them focus on giving love instead of always wanting things their own way. When both people think like this, their relationship becomes strong, peaceful, and full of beauty.

When couples build their life around God, their choices change. They are more likely to be patient during arguments. They are quicker to forgive. They show more grace when the other person makes a mistake. Instead of holding grudges, they try to love the way God teaches them to love. This makes their relationship feel safe and full of trust. It builds a deep respect that grows over time.

Daily faith practice also teaches couples how to serve one another with love and humility. They begin to understand that love isn't just a feeling; it is something they show through their actions. Simple things like helping, listening, and being there for each other become a natural part of their relationship. These acts of love don't come from pressure or duty, but from hearts focused on God and each other's well-being. Because of that, their joy doesn't belong to just one of them; it belongs to both. Their love grows deeper and stronger, not from big moments, but from choosing to live it out every single day.

Faith also reminds couples that life has a bigger meaning. It is not just about daily stress, bills, or routines. It is about growing together as people and learning how to love better each day. When couples believe this, they become more patient with their own struggles and the struggles of their partner. They see hard times as a chance to grow, not just a problem to fix. This mindset keeps the relationship moving forward, even when things are not perfect.

Another strength of faith in a relationship is the ability to pray together. Prayer creates moments where both partners open their hearts and connect with God. In those moments, fear turns into hope, worry into peace, and selfishness into love. Praying together strengthens trust between them. It serves as a reminder that they're not alone, they have each other, and they are supported by a loving God who is always there.

When problems arise, as they always do, faith becomes a guiding light for the couple. Instead of pointing fingers or walking away, they ask, "What would love do?" Then, they search for answers. They turn to their faith and teachings to help them make the right choices. This approach brings peace in difficult times, showing that their relationship isn't built on feelings alone, but on a foundation of truth and trust.

Faith is not just about religion; it is also about how two people live with care, respect, and love. It is shown in the small things, "how they speak, how they listen, how they forgive." These little choices add up over time. They build a strong wall of support that protects the relationship during difficult moments. When both people live their faith, they lift each other higher. Spiritual values also help couples grow. No one is perfect, and everyone makes mistakes, but faith teaches that growth is always possible. With love, patience, and help from God, each person becomes better. When couples believe this, they are more gentle with each other. They help each other rise instead of tearing each other down. This brings joy to the relationship and helps it last for many years.

Moreover, forgiveness is one of the most powerful gifts in a relationship. Forgiving is not always easy, but it's always needed to protect your relationship and to live happily. When two people share their lives, mistakes are meant to happen. Therefore, harsh words might be spoken, promises might be broken, and feelings might get hurt. But when forgiveness is offered with a sincere heart, healing begins. The relationship doesn't just survive; it grows stronger than it was before. Forgiveness is more than just saying, "I'm sorry," or "It's okay." It is a deep choice from the heart. It means letting go of the anger and pain someone caused. It means choosing peace over revenge. It means not bringing up the mistake again to hurt the other person later. When partners truly forgive, they make room for healing and love to grow again.

In relationships, small and big offenses slowly build walls. One person may feel hurt and stop talking as much; the other might feel guilty and pull away. Over time, these unspoken feelings grow into distance. But forgiveness tears those walls down. It gently removes the barriers that hurt, pride, or fear may have built. It says, "I still believe in you. I still choose us." That kind of choice brings freedom to heal, to grow, and to love again without holding back.

Forgiveness brings peace while holding onto anger creates stress, distance, and sadness. It makes a home feel cold and full of tension. But when forgiveness happens, that tension begins to fade. Even in silence, there will be peace again. Forgiveness also helps with intimacy because when a couple is holding on to past mistakes, it becomes hard to be close. Physical touch may feel forced. Words of love may sound empty. But when forgiveness enters the relationship, the heart begins to soften.

Therefore, a relationship without forgiveness will not last long. There will be too much pressure, too many wounds, and not enough hope. But a relationship with forgiveness survives many issues. In the end, the power of forgiveness is not just in the words; it is in the actions that follow. It is in the choice to love again, to trust again, and to keep moving forward with grace and hope. A relationship filled with forgiveness is like a strong tree. It grows deep roots, stands firm when storms come, and blooms again with joy, even after seasons of pain. Forgiveness doesn't erase the past, but it gives the future a chance to grow, stronger and more beautiful than before.

Chapter 9:
Practical Strategies for Reconnection

Modern life is always busy for every person. Most couples start their day with alarms, eat breakfast in a hurry, and then spend the rest of the day working, running errands, and handling responsibilities. However, with so much going on in their lives, they often do not notice that their emotional connection is fading. This change does not happen suddenly; it is slow and quiet. At first, everything feels normal. But one day, they look up and realize they have grown distant without even meaning to. For some people, it is too late to realize things cannot be fixed, but others still have time and try to make things right.

Long workdays, constant meetings, traffic jams, and chores at home cause couples to fall into different routines instead of staying connected. Therefore, over time, this lack of closeness starts to feel normal. Many couples still live under the same roof, but their conversations become more about tasks than feelings. They talk about paying bills, planning schedules, but they stop talking about their emotions, dreams, or what has been on their minds. This emotional distance doesn't mean the relationship is over or that you should leave your partner. Instead, it just means that it's time to slow down, think about what is missing, and start reconnecting in small and caring ways.

One of the easiest ways to fix disconnection in a relationship is often the most overlooked, which is spending simple moments together. You do not always need a fancy vacation or a big date night. What matters most are the small things you do often. Sharing a cup of coffee in the morning, holding hands while shopping, or sending a kind message during a busy day helps you feel close again. These little actions show love and attention, and they help build a stronger emotional bond. When two people regularly share the small, everyday moments of life then they build a strong emotional connection. These quiet routines, like talking while cooking or sitting together at the end of the day to help heal each other. It also helps the couple stay close and feel the connection with each other, even when life is stressful or with busy routines.

Therefore, consider doing simple things like making the bed together in the morning. It only takes a few minutes, but doing it side by side shows kindness and love. It might lead to a quick laugh, a small chat, or just the feeling of working as a team. It is a short, fun moment, but it brings back memories of why they fell in love in the first place. However, text messages might seem small thing, but when someone writes them with love, they become a very meaningful thing. A short message like "Thinking of you" or "Hope your meeting went well" is not just about the words. It shows the other person that they matter, even in the middle of a busy day. These little moments do not take much time, but they help build love and closeness over time.

Another good habit is relaxing together at the end of the day. Some couples make it a routine to sit on the couch, put their phones away, and just talk. It is not important to have deep conversations every time, but sometimes, it can be simple discussions, and they should have genuine feelings. You may ask questions like, "What made you smile today?" or "What was the hardest part of your day?" or something else, like simple questions, as this helps keep the connection strong. It is not about how long you talk, but how often you do it and how much you truly care. However, the best part is that none of these habits needs a lot of effort. Building a strong connection with your partner might not feel like a big job, but it becomes easy when you do it with true love and real feelings. Trying to create huge romantic gestures every week will actually lead to disappointment or exhaustion. Instead, it's the small, everyday efforts that slowly build a strong relationship, which handle life's stresses.

For couples with children, even five undistracted minutes after the kids go to bed makes a difference. A quiet moment on the porch, a shared laugh over a funny video, or reminiscing about a favorite vacation renew closeness without adding to the to-do list.

Therefore, even simple tasks bring people closer when they do them together. Folding laundry side by side gives you a chance to talk, share music, or just enjoy each other's presence. Moreover, washing the dishes while your partner dries them becomes a small habit that brings you closer. These everyday activities, when shared, become a reminder of partnership, not just chores.

I'm sharing the five easiest ways for couples that will help create a close connection with your partner:

- Before the day starts, take out five to ten minutes of time. You may just relax and drink coffee together while planning the day ahead, or simply sit close on the couch before the day begins. It does not matter what you do, but what matters is that you start the day feeling connected.

- Send a message during the day that is not about work or household chores. You may try saying something like, "I heard our song today and it made me smile." These quick messages remind each other that your relationship is about more than just handling responsibilities.

- Pick a regular evening routine. It could be ten minutes to talk about your day, watch a funny video together, or just lie on the bed and chat. These small moments help reduce the distance that daily stress creates.

- Instead of splitting tasks, try doing any one task as a team. Therefore, you may try washing dishes, cooking a meal, or cleaning out the garage as a team builds teamwork and opens space for natural conversation.
- Create a small weekly fun plan. It could be making pancakes on Sundays, playing cards or board games on Friday nights, or walking the dog every Saturday morning. Doing something fun together regularly gives you both something to look forward to and helps you build a shared routine.

However, these habits are simple and helpful ways to build a great connection with your partner. It helps couples get back to the basics of staying connected. Just like watering a plant, these little steps are not an instant way to fix everything in your relationship, but they will definitely help to build a connection gradually. Additionally, consistency helps a relationship grow, even with the busyness of everyday life. When reconnecting becomes a regular part of life instead of a chore, couples start to see each other not just as people who share chores or raise kids together, but as partners, lovers, and friends. The distance that once felt big starts to shrink, one small moment at a time.

In the end, the question is not "Do we have time?" but "Can we make space for each other in our busy lives?" When the answer is yes, even in small ways, that's when everyday habits turn into acts of love.

However, relationships grow distant over time, even when both partners still care for each other. This distance does not happen all at once, but it builds up slowly, often without anyone noticing. The pressure of daily life, like busy work schedules or personal stress, causes couples to lose the closeness they once had. At first, the change seems small, like a little less time spent together or fewer moments of affection. But if no one in your relationship notices such changes, then the relationship gap grows faster.

Therefore, there are signs that show a couple is growing apart, like less hugging or touching, getting annoyed more easily, or avoiding deep conversations. For example, when partners stop physical touch with each other, like holding hands, hugging, or kissing, it is a clear sign that something might be missing in their connection. It is easy to ignore these small changes, especially when both people are busy with work or family. But if they are not addressed, emotional distance becomes harder to stop later on. However, when couples start to feel emotionally distant, the first step is to notice it. The next step is to do something about it. There are many simple ways to feel close again. It does not always take big changes, but just small, thoughtful actions that help bring partners back together.

One of the best ways to reconnect is by having open and honest discussions. Setting aside some time every day to have a discussion with each other is a good first step. This does not mean you have to fix problems right away. It just means asking something like, "How have you been feeling?" and really listening to them is a good way. It gives both people a chance to tell their real feelings and thoughts in the safest way, without being judged or cut off.

Another simple but powerful way to feel closer again is by showing gratitude. Taking a moment to say "thank you" for the small things your partner does, like making breakfast or buying groceries, helps remind both of you how much you matter to each other. It is easy to overlook these little actions, but noticing them brings the spark back into the relationship. Moreover, listening is very important as well. Sometimes, partners stop truly listening because they are too busy or distracted. But making time to listen carefully, without cutting the other person off or looking at your phone, helps bring back closeness. It shows your partner that their feelings matter and that you care enough to really hear what they have to say.

Sometimes, couples need to plan time to be close. When life gets busy, it is easy to forget about physical closeness. That is why setting time aside for each other really helps. A planned date night or a quiet moment alone reminds both partners of their connection. These moments help the relationship feel special again, even when things are hectic. However, bringing back emotional and physical closeness takes effort, but it does not have to be hard. The main part is to do small, caring things often. These do not need to be big or take a lot of time. Sometimes, the little things, like sending a message to say you are thinking of your partner or holding hands while watching TV, make the biggest difference.

Additionally, building closeness means being intentional. Couples should make simple habits that bring them together, like turning off their phones during dinner or going for a walk each evening. It is about choosing to spend time with each other, even on busy days. These small actions help keep the connection strong and stop emotional distance from growing. Over time, these simple habits become part of the relationship. They help couples stay connected and remind them of the love they share. The more often partners practice these small acts of kindness, the stronger their bond becomes. Therefore, making connection a regular part of life, couples rebuild intimacy, even if they have been apart for a while.

Sometimes, couples need to change how they spend time together. Instead of always doing the same daily routine, it is helpful to try something new. This could be starting a hobby together, like cooking a new recipe or gardening with your partner. Doing new things gives partners a chance to work as a team and share fresh experiences. These actions help build a stronger connection. Another way to stay close is by surprising each other with small, kind gestures. These do not have to be big, like buying a gift or planning a trip. A short note, a small treat, or a surprise date night show your partner that you still care. Even little surprises make a big difference and remind each other that you're loved and appreciated.

Having simple routines together also helps keep the bond strong. This could be drinking coffee together every morning or watching a favorite show on the weekend. These small, repeated moments create comfort and closeness. When couples have something to enjoy together each week, it helps them feel more connected. Bringing back emotional and physical closeness is not just about fixing problems. It is about caring for the relationship in small, steady ways that keep it strong over time. With regular effort, by being present, listening well, and showing love in everyday actions, couples rebuild their connection. These small steps do not require big changes, but over time, they add up and help couples grow closer and handle life's challenges together.

Chapter 10:
Navigating Success as a Team

In every strong relationship, working together as a team is the secret to success. When two people help each other, they do much more than if they were on their own. By combining their strengths, avoiding confusion, and offering support, they reach their shared goals. However, teamwork not only makes hard times easier but also builds trust, respect, and unity. When partners support each other, it lowers stress and creates a space where both people grow together.

Moreover, real teamwork means both people care about each other's growth. Both partners have their dreams and aspirations, and it is necessary to support them. A healthy relationship does not require one person's dreams to die for the other's success. Rather, the couple supports each other for mutual growth. Suppose one partner wants to open a bakery, and the other wants to become a nurse. They could create a routine that could be favorable towards both objectives. So, for example, the nursing student could help their partner on weekends, while the baker would adjust their hours based on the other one's schedule. In that way, they are not just doing for their own dreams, but together.

Helping each other does not only mean giving sweet compliments. It also means showing love through actions. Someone could help with chores or give the other person plenty of time to work on a project. This kind of support from one partner tells both that they love one another. It gives a feeling that one understands and appreciates the other. When both partners give and receive, their bond strengthens. No one has to sacrifice his or her goal. They mutually complement each other in moving forward into the future.

Additionally, respect is also a very important part of a healthy relationship. It means listening, being kind, and making sure both people feel safe and important. Without respect, small issues quickly turn into big arguments. For example, one person might like to handle money in a certain way. They may enjoy saving most of it and being careful with spending. But the other person might have a different style. They might prefer to spend money on things they enjoy or feel are important, even if it means saving less. These different ways of managing money lead to misunderstandings if they don't talk and make a plan together.

However, if there is no respect, this difference leads to conflict. But when both people respect each other, they talk calmly, understand each other's views, and come up with a plan that works for both of them. Respect also means valuing each other's time and personal space. Life gets busy over time, and everyone needs time for themselves. If one person often cancels plans or does not respect their partner's needs, then they might end up hurting their feelings. But when both partners make time for each other and understand each other's needs, they avoid problems. Respect helps keep the relationship strong, even when life feels stressful.

Trust and respect are the most important parts of any strong relationship. In a healthy relationship, both people know they depend on each other, not just for help, but also for honesty and fairness. Trust takes time to build. It grows when both people show they are dependable, consistent, and care about each other. When both people respect each other's personal choices and differences, they make a place where both grow. For example, if one person is going through a tough time, the other will offer help and support without judging them. This respect helps both people feel important and confident, which makes it easier to face problems together and enjoy successes as a team.

Moreover, couples also need to know how to compromise. This means finding a solution that makes both people happy. For example, one person may like the house to be very clean, while the other does not mind a little mess. Instead of fighting about it, they can make a plan, like cleaning up a little each night and doing a bigger clean on the weekend. When couples compromise, both people feel heard and respected.

Another important part of teamwork in a relationship is solving problems together. Every couple has disagreements from time to time, but what really matters is how they deal with them. Instead of blaming each other, strong couples focus on finding solutions. They ask themselves, "How should we solve this problem together?" By thinking this way, they help keep the relationship calm and reduce stress. This approach helps them work as a team, no matter the challenge. Moreover, it also helps when couples have shared values and goals. When both people are working toward the same future, the relationship has purpose. Whether it is about saving money, starting a family, or building a business, sharing goals brings people closer. Working toward a goal gives couples something to focus on during hard times. It helps them remember why they are in it together.

Additionally, a helpful way for couples to build shared goals is by talking about the future, which some people call "vision casting." This means having conversations about what you want your life to be like, where you want to live, and the big moments you hope to experience together. These talks turn dreams into real plans. When couples dream and plan together, it creates excitement and trust between them. It also shows that both people are committed to going on the same journey and working toward the same future.

However, to keep teamwork strong, couples should always think about the bigger picture. Life brings challenges, but when partners focus on their shared dreams, they stay motivated to keep going. Instead of arguing or giving up when things get hard, they support each other and face tough times together. Each person has something special to offer, like different strengths, ideas, and energy. When they work as a team, they become even stronger.

Therefore, over time, this kind of teamwork builds a strong connection between two people. When they help each other, show respect, have honest conversations, and set goals together, it creates a deep bond. It is not just about reaching success, but it is about building a loving, supportive relationship that handles any challenges that come their way.

In the end, teamwork turns love into something lasting. It becomes a partnership where both people feel seen, supported, and appreciated. Their life together becomes meaningful, not just because of the good times, but because of how they have been facing everything side by side. A relationship built on teamwork is not just strong, it is full of hope, joy, and shared purpose.

Once a couple builds strong teamwork, then they are prepared for whatever life brings. However, life is not always easy. It is full of surprises, struggles, and tough choices. Even with the best plans, unexpected things happen. When a couple faces these moments together, as a team, they grow stronger. Instead of letting problems push them apart, they use those challenges to grow closer. They create emotional safety, which means each person feels supported and not alone. It brings comfort to know someone is always there for you. This kind of support builds strength, especially during hard times.

Additionally, difficult moments look different for every couple. It could be losing a job, dealing with illness, money problems, or family issues. These tests are not just about each person's strength, but also how strong the relationship is. Couples who go through these things together often come out stronger. They talk openly, share their worries, and help each other carry the weight. Instead of trying to handle everything alone, they lean on each other. One partner might feel tired or weak, while the other steps in to help more. That back-and-forth support is what teamwork really means, especially when life gets tough.

Therefore, encouragement is very important during these hard times. It is not just about saying things like "you'll be fine." True encouragement often comes through actions. One partner might do more chores when the other is too tired, or they might cook a meal, offer a hug, or just sit quietly together. These small, caring actions mean a lot. They show real love and support. Sometimes, encouragement means helping your partner believe in themselves again. It is reminding them that they are strong and capable. These moments build trust, comfort, and the feeling of being truly cared for.

However, it is just as important to celebrate the good times, too. When something good happens, even if it is something small, it helps to pause and enjoy it together. Maybe one partner finishes a project, gets a promotion, or reaches a personal goal. Taking time to recognize that win, even with a kind word or shared dinner, adds joy to the relationship. Celebrating wins, whether they are big or small, helps couples feel valued and encouraged. These happy moments bring joy and create good memories that give them strength during tough times. They also remind the couple that their journey together matters and is worth it.

Additionally, celebration helps bring balance to a relationship. Life is not just about solving problems or getting through hard times, but it is also about enjoying good moments and having fun together. When couples make time for both the tough times and the happy times, their relationship feels more complete and healthier. For example, if one person reaches a fitness goal or gets a new job, the other cheers them on and shares their joy. This makes the person feel seen, supported, and important. When both people feel noticed and celebrated, their emotional bond becomes stronger. Over time, these happy moments turn into special memories. They become part of the couple's shared story, a story not just about facing challenges, but also about growing together, feeling proud of each other, and building a life filled with love and joy.

Therefore, making decisions together is an important part of handling life's ups and downs. Couples face many choices in life, like how to manage money, where to live, and how to spend their time. These decisions are sometimes stressful or confusing. But when both people talk honestly and listen kindly, they find answers that work for both of them. Sometimes, one person may think in a more logical way, while the other is more focused on feelings, and that is perfectly okay. These different ways of thinking will actually be helpful. When both sides are respected, the couple makes better and more balanced choices. For example, one partner might be good at planning steps and solving problems, while the other makes sure they do not forget how the decision might affect people emotionally. By working together and combining their strengths, couples make smarter and more caring decisions.

However, working as a team does not mean always agreeing. Differences are normal and even healthy. What matters is how those differences are handled. Couples who trust each other disagree without hurting the relationship. They do not try to "win" arguments. Instead, they try to understand each other and find a solution. They speak with care, stay calm, and focus on solving the problem and not blaming each other. This respectful way of handling differences keeps the relationship strong, even when tough choices need to be made.

As time goes on, couples who work as a team, through both good and bad, build something truly strong. Therefore, trust grows with every moment of support. This trust does not come just from words, but from actions. It shows in keeping promises, handling tough feelings gently, and always being there. With time, the relationship becomes a safe space. Both people feel free to be themselves, knowing they are accepted and supported no matter what.

In the end, couples who keep choosing teamwork, again and again, build a strong and lasting relationship. Their story is shaped by support, shared dreams, and deep trust. Yes, there are challenges along the way, but what makes their story special is how they face those challenges side by side. Through working together, they learn not just how to survive the hard times, but how to grow and succeed. Their love becomes a steady and reliable force that helps them keep moving forward, no matter what life brings. They build a life that is full of meaning, strength, and happiness.

Conclusion

A lot of people work very hard to become successful. They use up a lot of their time and energy trying to reach their goals. But being truly successful should not mean losing your family, your partner, or the people you love. In this book, we talked about how chasing success will be hard, especially for romantic relationships.

Therefore, people who work very hard to meet deadlines, travel constantly for business, and always seem busy, tend to find it difficult to find time for their loved ones. Life almost feels like a race. Yet, with a busy schedule, it is still possible to get on successful career paths while at the same time developing a happy and loving relationship.

Each chapter in this book shares stories of real couples facing these challenges. These stories helped explain ideas in a simple and clear way. They also reminded us that no relationship is perfect. Every couple has problems. What matters most is how they handle those problems together. Some couples work on spending more time together. Others set clear rules about work and home.

Additionally, empathy is an important point of this book, which means trying to understand how your partner feels. It means caring about their emotions and showing support. You do not just listen, you feel with them. Simple things like kind words, a hug, or showing up when they need you build a stronger bond. These little things matter a lot in love.

Nowadays, work and home life often mix together. Many people check emails at night, take phone calls during dinner, or keep thinking about work even when they are at home. This makes it hard for couples to connect. We talked about ways to create better boundaries. That might mean turning off your phone during meals or setting a rule about no work talk after a certain hour. Spending even just ten minutes a day really listening to each other makes a big difference.

Furthermore, we also talked about how important it is to support each other's dreams. It is not about giving up your own goals. It is about helping each other grow. When you support your partner's dreams, you build a relationship based on respect and trust. When one person wins, both people win as a couple, and when one person struggles, the other is there to help.

We have also mentioned long-distance relationships in this book. Whether the distance lasts a few months or a few years, love still survives. We shared tips like regular messages, video calls, shared routines, and having plans for the future. These things help people stay close, even when they're far apart.

Another important subject was parenting while working. Many couples are raising children and also building their careers. This is not easy. We talked about ways to make sure children feel loved and get enough attention. Simple things like eating meals together, bedtime stories, weekend outings, and showing love in front of your kids help a lot. Children feel safe when they see their parents working as a team.

Moreover, for couples who feel like they don't have enough time together, we suggested easy steps. You should schedule time for just the two of you, just like you would for a meeting. You should say no to extra work when it is not truly needed, and you should use small daily habits, like having morning coffee together or taking evening walks, to stay connected. It is not about how much time you spend, but how meaningful that time is.

Furthermore, we also discussed the importance of faith in a relationship. Faith instills resilience, creating a safe haven for couples amidst life's inevitable storms. When partners share spiritual beliefs, their bond deepens, allowing them to navigate challenges together rather than apart. Following that, we talked about healing a relationship when it feels broken. Every couple has ups and downs. But with honesty, time, and a desire to fix things, love grows again. Some couples find help through therapy. Others write in journals, go on trips together, or simply have long, honest talks. Even when things feel stuck, change is possible if both people want to try.

Throughout this book, we kept the writing simple and clear. You could read it during lunch, before bed, or while traveling. We wanted every reader to feel supported and understood. Whether you are newly married or have been together for a long time, this book will help you build something lasting and full of love.

As we reach the end of this book, we want to remind you of something important: success is not just about money, promotions, or finishing goals. Real success is having someone to share your life with. When you come home tired, it matters who is waiting for you. When life feels stressful, knowing that you are not alone gives you strength. Small daily habits make a big difference. Showing that you're thankful to them, showing patience, or taking time to really listen, all these little things help love grow. They build trust and keep the relationship strong, even when life is busy.

The best relationships give you peace and strength. They help you grow and chase your dreams. A good partner is someone who encourages you, supports you, and loves you no matter what. That's the real goal—not just success, but shared success. It's about enjoying life with someone who believes in you and stands by your side.

In the end, the most meaningful kind of success is the one you share with someone else. It is not just about reaching your goals alone; it is about having someone to celebrate with when you get there. A strong relationship is like a safe place, where you can be yourself without fear. It gives you comfort during hard times and joy during the good ones. When you have someone who listens to you, believes in you, and helps you stay grounded, everything feels more balanced.

That kind of love doesn't just happen by accident. It takes effort, honesty, and time. It means choosing to make space for your partner, even when life is busy. It means checking in, showing up, and not taking each other for granted. Work and ambition are important, but so is love, care, and connection.

As you move forward in your journey, remember that true success includes the people who walk with you. Never forget to make time for love, and never stop showing your partner that you're thankful to them. And most of all, do not forget that life feels richer when you are not walking the path alone. That's the kind of success worth building.

References / Sources

1. How to Manage Love and Career. Retrieved April 2, 2025:

   https://psychcentral.com/relationships/tips-to-maintain-a-work-life-balance-during-a-relationship?utm

2. Wikipedia.org; Wikimedia Foundation, Inc:

   https://en.wikipedia.org/wiki/The_Five_Love_Languages

3. How to Balance Your Career and Relationship. (2021, May 20):

   https://www.growingself.com/how-to-balance-your-career-and-relationship/

4. Equilibrium of personal life, professional life, and family life. Retrieved April 9, 2025, from Wikipedia.org website:

   https://en.wikipedia.org/wiki/Work%E2%80%93life_balance

5. Strong, deep, or close association or acquaintance between two or more people. Wikipedia.org; Wikimedia Foundation, Inc:

   https://en.wikipedia.org/wiki/Interpersonal_relationship

6. Sign #1 of a Healthy Relationship: Partners Support Each Other's Opportunities for Growth. (2015, September 11)

   https://www.mandiroarke.com/read-the-blog/2015/9/11/sign-1-

of-a-hssealthy-relationship-partners-support-each-others-opportunities-for-growth

7. Long-Distance-Relationships Advice: How to Make it Work. (April 29, 2025)

https://www.thecut.com/article/long-distance-relationships-advice-how-to-make-it-work.html

8. 10 Quick & Powerful Ways to Reconnect in a Busy Marriage. (May 14, 2025)

https://www.maverickmarriagetherapy.com/post/10-marriage-reconnection-tips

9. *Husband and Wife: Be a Team.* (2025, April 14)

https://heart2heartwithsyedalihaider.com/husband-and-wife-be-a-team/